THE HEALTH PRACTITIONER'S JOURNEY

Your Ultimate Four-Stage Guide to a Successful and Financially Rewarding Career

THE HEALTH PRACTITIONER'S JOURNEY

Your Ultimate Four-Stage Guide to a Successful and Financially Rewarding Career

Michael Kenihan

Foreword by Professor Karim M. Khan AO

Social Star
103/25 Gipps Street,
Collingwood, Vic, 3066
socialstar.com.au

This first edition published by Social Star in 2024.
Copyright © Michael Kenihan 2024

All rights reserved. Without limiting the rights under copyright reserved above, no part of this publication may be reproduced, stored in or introduced into a retrieval system, or transmitted, in any form or by any means (electronic, mechanical, photocopying, recording or otherwise) without the prior written permission of the publishers of this book.

Typeset in Cardea OTCE and New Zen by WorkingType (Australia).

Printed in Australia by IngramSpark, part of the Ingram Content Group.

Paperback ISBN 978-0-6450386-4-4
eBook ISBN 978-0-6450386-5-1

 A catalogue record for this book is available from the National Library of Australia

*For my wife Sarah Jane Watson
and our four children, Sebastian, Madelaine,
Lucinda and Charlie.*

What health professionals are saying about *The Health Practitioner's Journey*:

"If only I had this book when I was starting my sports medicine journey — it would have saved me making lots of mistakes along the way. Every health practitioner would benefit from Mike Kenihan's wisdom."

Peter Brukner OAM, D Sc, MBBS, FACSP
Sport and Exercise Medicine Physician
Professor of Sports Medicine, La Trobe University

"It's wise, it's practical — it's essential ... I'm sure this book will be much loved by the next generations of healthcare practitioners."

Professor Karim M. Khan AO
Former Sports and Exercise Medicine Physician
Former Editor-in-chief of the *British Journal of Sports Medicine*
Co-author of *Clinical Sports Medicine*

"*The Health Practitioner's Journey* should be embraced by all — aspiring first-year students through to seasoned health practitioners. Read this book and keep it as an ongoing resource."

Cris Massis

Board Member, Osteopathy Australia

Chief Executive, Australian Physiotherapy Association (2011-19)

"Michael's sage advice 'Your value as a practitioner resides in your knowledge and not in your job' can support a lifetime of career and life changes. Have Michael's book on hand over the years and refer to it often ..."

Dr Trish Wisbey-Roth

Olympic/Specialist Sports Physiotherapist FASMA, FACP, MAPA

"*The Health Practitioner's Journey* is relevant for our specific industry: practical, full of good clear examples, contains specific benchmarks for clinical practice, and these tools alone make it worth purchasing."

Paul Coburn

Former Richmond Football Club Physiotherapist

Contents

Foreword	1
Preface	5
Introduction: The Health Practitioner's Journey	7

1.0 STAGE ONE: Building Your List — Clinical Excellence — 11
- 1.1 Who is Stage One For? — 13
- 1.2 What is Clinical Excellence? — 18
- 1.3 Why is Clinical Excellence Important? — 54
- 1.4 What Else Do I Need to Achieve Clinical Excellence? — 56

2.0 STAGE TWO: Owning Your List — Commercial Success — 65
- 2.1 Who is Stage Two For? — 68
- 2.2 What is Commercial Success? — 70
- 2.3 Why is Commercial Success Important? — 109
- 2.4 What Else Do I Need to Achieve Commercial Success? — 112

3.0 STAGE THREE: Leading Your List — Maximise Equity — 117
- 3.1 Who is Stage Three For? — 120
- 3.2 What is Maximising Equity? — 124
- 3.3 Why is Maximising Equity Important? — 202
- 3.4 What Else Do I Need to Maximise Equity? — 205

4.0 STAGE FOUR: Selling Your List
— Leverage Equity   207
    4.1 Who is Stage Four For?   209
    4.2 What is Leveraging Equity?   213
    4.3 Why is Leveraging Equity Important?   228
    4.4 What Else Do I Need to Leverage Equity?   229

5.0 Harvesting Knowledge
    5.1 What is Harvesting Knowledge?   231
    5.2 My Journey   235
    5.3 What Have Others Done to Harvest
          Their Knowledge?   241

Appendices
    1. Achieving Your Career Objectives   251
    2. Achieving Your Business Objectives   265

Acknowledgements   283
About the Author   285
Index   287

Foreword

This is a brilliant book for many, many early- and mid-career health practitioners. As you will quickly gather, the book outlines four stages of the health practitioner's journey.

When I first met Michael, he had been at the top of junior sport as a high jumper, he was already renowned as an empathetic and skilled clinician whose patient list quickly ballooned beyond the hours in his working week. At this time, he was at Stage Two in his health practitioner's journey, as outlined in this book. We shared an eight-hour drive to the 1987 Australian Sports Medicine Conference and I realised — even then — that I was privileged to be sharing time with a very special individual.

Already by 1987, Mike Kenihan cared deeply about patients, his colleagues, and the staff who supported the clinicians. He saw above the ever-present petty workplace politics. He was clearly already an inspiring leader.

I was aware of his move into clinic leadership; his practice group expanded and provided quality care. Mike moved into major national leadership positions. During that phase, our paths crossed again when I was Editor of the *British Journal of Sports Medicine*. He was Australia's delegate for FIMS (Fédération Internationale de Médecine du Sport), the largest international sports medicine federation — a terrific choice. At this time, he was serving the community and moving through Stages Three and Four of the health practitioner's journey. Mike is a pioneer and paved the way. This book is a map for success, or an app — depending on what you prefer!

This book surprised me in how much practical wisdom Mike could pack into the pages. I love the synthesis: clinical expertise, business savvy (clearly explained), organisational processes, and life experience. I can't do justice to all the practical tips in each chapter, but one stellar example is the eight ways of ensuring your consultation is highly effective for both patient and clinician. This book is both a how-to manual (which makes it very attractive) and a manifesto that human values go alongside career development and being paid appropriately. Not a case of either/or! How to be a good person first, and also a caring clinician, a responsible work colleague, a leader and to have work-life-financial-stability balance in your chosen career.

I'm confident readers will love the logical structure. Why do the Four Stages exist? What does each one involve? Why are they important? How does one progress to the top of each stage and beyond? (You can see the clinician in Mike — he 'progresses' the reader through their career the way he would progress a patient back to return to sport at the highest level!) The diagrams are very helpful too

— they illustrate important concepts — most of which are MK originals. I can see those original concepts doing well on social media as this book jumps off the shelves.

One of Mike's key messages is to be proactive — don't wait for things to happen; one has to make them happen. How to make them happen is right here in this book. Don't waste time if a short gap arises between patients. Tidy up, or call a patient back, or update a referrer. But not in a jumpy manner — in keeping with the systematic goal-setting Mike suggests you take your time to do.

"Today a reader and tomorrow a leader." Of course, Mike is a wide reader and he shares the best of the books that have influenced his actions. Not just his thinking but his behaviours. You'll find Stephen Covey (from *The Seven Habits of Highly Effective People*), Robert Cialdini (*Influence: The Psychology of Persuasion*) and the Heath Brothers (*Made to Stick*) in this book — people who have influenced the world but who find it hard to crack into a health professional curriculum.

A small proportion of clinicians take the journey from being a provider to leading a multi-partner practice. Fewer lead in a large multidisciplinary setting. And fewer still have been part of a national corporation that manages more than 350 clinicians and staff. Mike Kenihan combines this rare experience with his thoughtful, humble and grounded values — and pours all this into *The Health Practitioner's Journey*. He shares more than a map — he has created the 'Lonely Planet' guide for the journey that will allow clinicians to function at their highest level.

Every graduating health practitioner needs to read this — otherwise, how can they decide whether their journey is right for them or not? Those who wish to build or buy their own practice need to read this book. It can save you a lifetime of journeying, either aimlessly or, perhaps, even in the opposite direction to where you should be going. This book will help guide you to the destination: working in a role you love, with people who are of a similar mindset, where your worth is rewarded, and you have the freedom to make choices.

It's wise, it's practical — it's essential. Kudos, Mike Kenihan, from all who have been fortunate to be in your circle; I count myself among those. Thank you for sharing your gift of experience and knowledge widely. I'm sure this book will be much loved by the next generations of healthcare practitioners.

Professor Karim M. Khan AO
Former Sports and Exercise Medicine Physician
Former Editor-in-chief of the *British Journal of Sports Medicine*
Co-author of *Clinical Sports Medicine*

Preface

This book is for anyone who sees allied health or indeed professional practice as their chosen career. Should you be a new graduate or someone towards the end of your career, you will find yourself somewhere along the path of the practitioner journey in this book.

Over my career I have worked as a practitioner in almost every element of clinical practice and practice businesses from working in elite sports, suburban practice, team sport, as an owner, a purchaser, developer of allied health and multidisciplinary practices, as well as working in the corporate environment. I was there from the beginning when allied health businesses began to be purchased and corporatised. I see that trend continuing.

The perspective I gained on my journey afforded me many opportunities to learn and grow. Within those practices I developed a role as mentor and manager and was able to share many principles I had learnt with others. I worked closely with many young practitioners and assisted them to understand how to improve their practice and grow their patient following. I also worked with those who operate the business or desire to be a part of a network or want to sell to a corporate. I attempted to motivate practitioners to see value in their career and to seek new possible opportunities in practice.

Now that I'm in the latter years of my working life, I am driven to share my thoughts and ideas with others. Perhaps this book will allow me to spread my message more widely and provide the opportunity to speak as one to many, more so than speaking one-to-one or one-to-a-few.

I invite you to take the journey just as I did and to see how your career can develop and blossom in the hope this provides you enormous satisfaction, as it has for me.

Michael Kenihan

President of the Australian Sports Medicine Federation

Order of Fellows

November 2023

Introduction

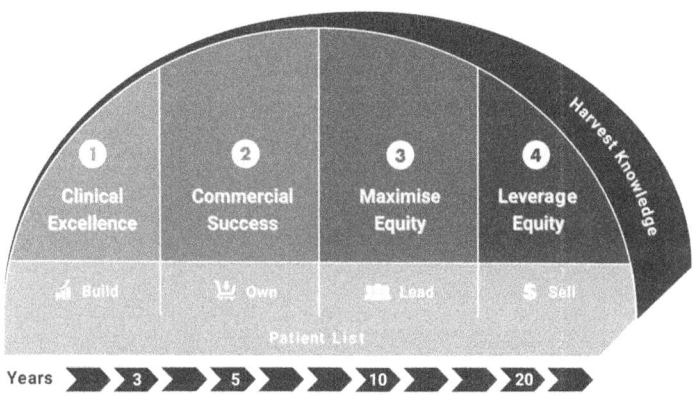

Figure 1: The Health Practitioner's Journey

The Health Practitioner's Journey is based upon my experience as a practitioner who started a professional career as a sports physio, then worked in multidisciplinary practices, becoming a manager, then an owner and developer of allied health businesses. I have used the timeline from that journey as the basis and structure of this book, breaking up my career into what I'm going to call four stages that are represented in the above diagram. This covers my career from graduation day up until now.

The four stages are:

1. Clinical Excellence

2. Commercial Success

3. Maximise Equity

4. Leverage Equity

The diagram shows a linear path with years indicated because that was my path. However, I do not see the time fragments as set in stone, and the time taken to achieve milestones may be shorter or longer than what I have indicated. I have known some practitioners who have paused their career at clinical excellence or commercial success, which is absolutely fine. They are happy with their work and are successful in it and pausing there has suited them. Also note that at the completion of stage four there is more. I have included a chapter that I call Harvesting Knowledge, where practitioners have used the skills learnt on the journey to do different activities in their career, just as I have done. It is added in 3D because it is relevant and sits behind each of the four sections, which I will explain when we get there.

I have also used the metaphor of the list as the path. When you begin practice you *build* a list of patients to treat. As you become more competent, you begin to *own* that patient list. That means you have loyal patients who will follow you and ask for you when they need assistance. As you continue in practice and your list becomes larger, you develop commercial success. The next stage is to *lead* your patient list, which means using new skills to engage others to work with you in a business that you might commence. Finally, the list you have nurtured, and taught others to do the same, becomes an asset that you can *sell* when that time comes for you.

By dividing this book into stages, I am hoping it will be read by practitioners who find themselves in any of these stages, i.e. you might want to start reading at the beginning of stage two or stage three, for example. My consulting work both within corporate organisations and in practices I have personally owned has taught me that the principles of clinical excellence leading to commercial success, and then to managing the equity you are building, and then finally leveraging that equity into a profitable sale, may be stages you have been through or you are wanting to move towards from where you are now. As mentioned, I know many fulfilled practitioners who love clinical practice, are exceptional practitioners and are commercially successful without starting their own business. I hope this book adds something for them to consider in their careers as well.

Finally, my wish is that more people who enter professional health practice see that practice as a career worth continuing within. I hope this book assists you to see opportunities for yourself within that practice, or in the process of harvesting knowledge, which can be placed for good use, creating further opportunities for growth and success.

1.0 STAGE ONE

Building Your List — Clinical Excellence

The Health Practitioner's Journey™

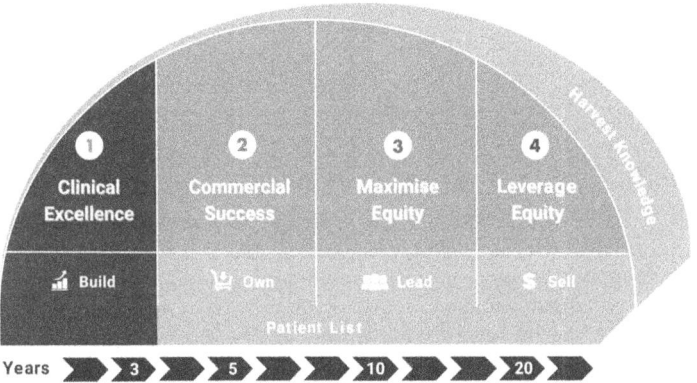

Clinical excellence should be the cornerstone of health practice.

1.1   Who is Stage One For?

When you graduate you will have a licence to learn, and this stage will assist you to develop your future career opportunities. Alternatively, your first few years in practice may not have delivered the skills and abilities you desired and hence this stage is also there for you.

When you graduate you may feel you have studied enough in your undergraduate years and that you need a rest from extra study, but the experience gained in the first years of treating patients will consolidate your knowledge and help to develop your skills. Accepting the input and guidance of those around you who have more experience, plus exploring how to be better by observing others and having mentors review how you are performing, is essential. These things will help you to develop clinical excellence as well as building your patient list.

Building your patient list while developing clinical excellence is not just for graduates, it also applies when you are recruited to a new job or when you move to a new practice. Seeing sufficient patients to learn more skills and develop your abilities is also crucial. Gaining help to develop will be particularly important and you should seek this help from your new practice principals, as they will not know the precise levels of your abilities when you commence with them.

Stage One covers the first three years of practice. Depending on the level of support for your learning and your level of engagement, you may progress quickly or more slowly. Hopefully, an increase in your productivity — based on application to learning and achieving a growing list of patients — will be the outcome over this period.

When we talk about therapist productivity, I believe it is a delicate subject that is often misunderstood. At its core, it is about caring for patients while controlling non-billable tasks that waste time and take you away from patient care.

For example, 10-15% of a therapist's time may be unproductive because of cumbersome documentation and administrative tasks. Such tasks may include poor digital record-keeping, mistakes with bookings, telephone interruptions and the like. To reduce the burden of these tasks, you should work with the reception or admin staff to streamline calls, check on the appointment diary to see why there are problems, or even discuss the practice software issues with the practice owner/manager.

I have a table that will assist you to be more productive:

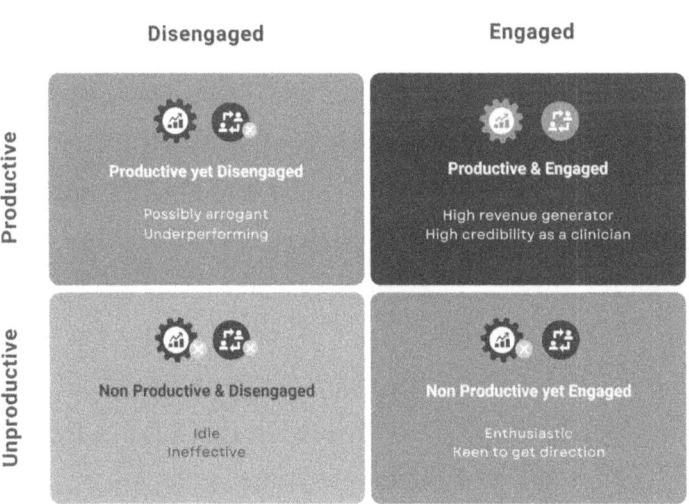

Figure 2: The Engagement Model

If you look at the above table, you will observe that this model identifies productivity and engagement. Why do I focus on engagement as well as productivity?

I believe that one cannot be productive without first being engaged. For example, there was a young clinician whom I was mentoring in his practice. He was not improving clinically and not achieving his commercial goals either. It was time for a meaningful conversation. I asked him why he wasn't improving and he explained that he was not really engaged in the process of care delivery. I suggested his patients felt that and therefore did not return for subsequent visits. After time and hard talk, he revealed that he did not think the situation would change for him. We discussed his options at the practice, and he related his interest in banking and finance. It was mutually agreed that he should pursue this interest and he left the practice. Twelve months later we caught up and he was studying finance and working part-time with a financial advisor learning the trade. He was incredibly happy. His disengagement as a health practitioner sabotaged his attempts to see more patients, earn more money and further his learning.

My working definition of productivity in clinical practice is firstly about being engaged to learn. In graduates this often involves having a passion for your practice. Secondly, it's about applying better reasoning, implementing treatment techniques, and understanding how to provide effective advice. These skills take time and some mentoring to develop. Make sure you seek assistance to develop these important skills to be more productive.

Referring back to the table when you are engaged and productive (top right quarter), you will be a higher revenue generator and attain high credibility as a clinician. Conversely, if we look at low engagement and low productivity (bottom left quarter), then we have someone who is mentally idle and ineffective with their treatments.

Do not despair if you feel you may not be in the most productive and engaged quadrant in this table. People will occupy any of the four quadrants at various times and sometimes it is best to have honest conversations with young clinicians, as I have outlined above. Doing so is a service to that clinician and not just a feedback session.

Here are the benefits of being engaged and productive:
- Your earning potential grows.
- Your clinical excellence improves.
- Your confidence and satisfaction will increase.
- Your balance of your time improves.
- You'll feel greater enthusiasm and engagement with patients.
- There will be greater opportunities to develop your relationships with other clinicians and to develop your career.

An example of the benefits of being engaged and productive is a young therapist named Sue. Sue commenced as a new graduate and worked under a supportive system of formal mentoring and development of clinical excellence. She attended tutorials and took the opportunity to observe more experienced practitioners. Provision of regular feedback on her performance with file reviews and case presentations to her mentors assisted her. She also set clear objectives for her learning and designated time to read articles and attend formal courses. Within two years Sue had identified a special interest in the treatment of lower limb injuries. Her practice was productive and she built her patient list up to 80%. This achievement increased her confidence and self-esteem, and she started to gain more direct referrals from the friends of patients she had treated and from her professional referrer network. It was gratifying to see that Sue was at ease when she worked and was a more effective and productive team member in the practice. And she soon had a full patient list.

1.2 What is Clinical Excellence?

Becoming clinically excellent is based on seven specific activities: Clinical Reasoning, Application of Clinical Reasoning, Training Processes, Time Management and Planning, Goal Setting, Effectiveness and Efficiency, and Essential Behaviours.

1.2.1 Clinical Reasoning

Understanding the importance of the consultation is the start to learning clinical reasoning. By this I mean understanding that the questions you ask, what you observe, and the findings both physical and mental from your examination, need to then have a rationale applied that will assist you to know what to do with what you find out.

The accepted way to approach the consultation is to use the SOAP approach:

Subjective exam — the questions that you ask about the person and their problem.

Objective exam — what you gain by observation, when you get the patient to move and by specific tests you administer.

Assessment — how you collate what you have learnt into a working diagnosis.

Plan and treatment — what treatment you intend to apply, advice you will give and any home routines or actions you prescribe.

The SOAP approach is fine but does not contain all the elements of a successful consultation. I like to expand the paradigm and base my approach on an eight-step model of selling. It may seem strange that I use the word *selling*, but it is worth explaining what I mean. Whatever you do, you are selling yourself, your service, your knowledge, and by doing this you will ensure that the patient will understand the shared goals you develop with them and be compliant with the treatment you will administer. This includes any techniques, advice, counselling, home activities or exercises that you might prescribe.

It is important to explain how the SOAP approach and the eight steps of selling work within the consultation. From my experience, if you join those two approaches to the consult you will find that the patient is more likely to provide more information and be more at ease as you pursue the questioning process. The consult should also come to a more productive conclusion.

Here's how the SOAP paradigm fits within the eight steps of selling:

1. Preparation

2. Rapport building

3. Analysis of needs (the S and O — subjective and objective examinations)

4. Development of solutions (the A — assessment)

5. Customisation of benefits (the P — plan)

6. Demonstration of value (the treatment)

7. Brief summary of your offering

8. Caring close

And here is a pictorial representation of this consult model:

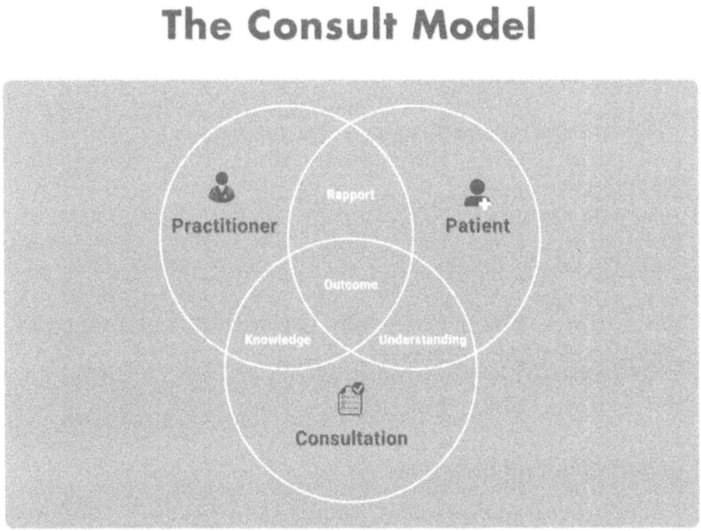

The Consult Model

Figure 3: The Consult Model

Let's now go through the eight steps of selling with the SOAP approach integrated:

1. Preparation

Being prepared to treat someone is important. I call the preparation a 'commercial behaviour' as there are things you should do even before the patient arrives. For example: Is the treatment room you are to use well organised? Is the plinth covering clean and hygienic? Do you have the things you will need in the treatment room/cubicle, so you do not have to exit and enter the room too many times during the consult? Are you ready to greet the patient with a friendly smile and direct eye contact? Was the patient referred to you or the practice? Have they been a past patient of the practice?

Try to learn as much as you can about this patient before the consult.

2. Rapport Building

The establishment of trust with the patient will be crucial to how well the consultation will go. Showing interest in the patient and their life is important for them to feel comfortable and receptive to what you may say or do.

Developing rapport nonverbally is important. Gestures, your sense of care, how you make the patient comfortable and how you address them are all important. Asking about their day, their job, their family will show that you are interested and will assist the patient to be more relaxed in your company. Listening intently and empathetically is essential. An effective way to show the depth of your listening is to repeat or reflect back to them what they might say. For example, if they describe their day or their stress, you can respond with: "Yes, that sounds stressful," or "It must be really difficult to manage that."

Noticing what the patient mentions while developing rapport is also helpful. An example could be how they like you to address them, e.g. their name may be John, however, if they say, "But everyone calls me Jack," then make a note so next time you call them Jack. Being liked is an important principle of social influence and is something that will assist in your consultation. But do avoid being overly familiar, of course.

3. Analysis of Needs

This step is the subjective and objective part of the SOAP approach. Asking open questions is a key to understanding and will get your patient talking and feeling more comfortable. Find out about what has happened to them and why they have come to see you. Ask them how they came to attend the clinic today. This is also valuable information for you to collate because it will assist you with developing/growing your list in the future (more on this topic later in this book).

Once you understand what has happened, it is good to ask what their expectation of treatment is (do not assume you know). What are their goals? Do they have something important to do or attend or compete at in the near future?

This will provide their expected timeline to recovery. Focus upon what the patient wants to achieve. This will help you to determine the urgency of this problem, which may have implications for the treatment.

The problem may not be obvious, so being sure to observe the patient and understand if they have had other treatments or clinicians treat them recently is good to know.

I remember working with an experienced sports physician for years. His name was Gary and he used to say that from when he greeted a patient until they sat down in his consult room, he had determined half of what he needed to know by closely observing how they moved, their facial expressions when they moved, and their overall demeanour.

4. Development of Solutions

This is the assessment part of the SOAP approach and involves a process of starting to engineer your patient's expectations. If they have an acute ankle injury and expect to be able to run a marathon in a week, or if they show extreme signs of stress due to performance anxiety, or exhibit an extremely emotional reaction to what is going on, then you will need to gently lower their expectations of what they may be able to achieve in the short-term.

Take the information you have, then design a treatment plan for them. If they have something particularly important to attend or do, then you will need to assess what is realistic to achieve. Under-promising and over-delivering is the best path to take. You may decide to refer your patient to a crisis management facility or a specialist for assistance if you fear for their mental health, or think what they have/are exhibiting is beyond your capability to treat at that time. A good referral to another discipline/practitioner can be as productive and helpful as a treatment from you.

5. Customisation of Benefits

This is the plan part of the SOAP approach. At this stage you will have designed the treatment/management that you intend to provide, and it is important to sell the benefits of what you intend to do. For example, saying something like: "If we provide this treatment, then you will feel better and be able to do more, even though you will not be able to do all that you want to do." Talk about the risks of not getting treatment or indeed of not following the treatment plan that you are suggesting. Point out to them what might happen if they don't follow the treatment plan.

A good example of this from my experience is Maddy. This young person presented with a badly sprained knee joint. She had a university exam coming up, plus was captain of the netball team, and the team was to compete in a final series. She was anxious about her exam and about her chances of competing at the netball finals. Maddy needed a plan that involved physical therapy, but also an appointment to see a psychologist to help her sort out the competing needs she had and how best she could cope. In the end she did not appreciate the need to follow through with the plan advised and competed when not ready, further injuring the knee. This put her out for the following season. Another result was that she wasn't in the best state for the exam and she only just passed. Being able to see into the future for patients is something that is part of the customising of benefits.

6. Demonstration of Value (the Treatment)

In this step you should emphasise the difference the treatment should make, then:

- Apply the treatment techniques/advice, counselling and products.
- Reassess the effect of your intervention by performing physical reassessment, observing the mood or confidence difference, and the level of satisfaction with the advice.
- Be confident with the reassessment, as there will be a strong placebo response if you convey confidence and belief in your treatment/management.
- Engineer your patient's expectation of the treatment by outlining how they may feel, e.g. they may be confused with the advice you have provided, and this is okay because they can clarify that with a call or message to you. They may also feel soreness where

you have applied the treatment, and this may linger for a day or two but will diminish.
- Provide extra information, e.g. a website for more information about their condition, a handout with exercises, or further information they can refer to — either paper or digital.

7. Brief Summary of Your Offering

This step is a process of recounting what you have discussed, observed and provided at the consultation. In short, repeat the advice you provided, what treatment you administered and why. Detail the instructions you have provided for your patient to work on at home and outline the intensity of the effort you require. Patients are often inclined to do more than asked because they often believe more is better.

8. Caring Close

To finish your time with the patient, it is always important to make sure you clarify both your and the patient's expectations. Remind them about what you think the problem is and how you intend to assist them. Describe what future treatment may involve and the frequency of visits they may need to have. Ensure you discuss the next visit time with them before they go back to reception. And make sure they understand how important it is to comply with the treatment/advice you have provided.

Your patient should have a clear idea of what the

diagnosis is, what you have recommended to help them, and how they are to progress from then on. Ensure you provide a fond and caring farewell.

1.2.2 Application of Clinical Reasoning

Once you have completed the consultation, made the observations from your examination, reasoned solutions, and shown the benefit of your treatment interventions, then you will have demonstrated value to the patient. I will now discuss how you can more effectively apply your clinical reasoning under three main headings: Advice and Messaging, Therapy, and Actions and Behaviours.

Advice and Messaging

What you say to a patient is immensely powerful, yet your patient is unlikely to remember everything that you have advised. It is common nature that this will be the situation.

Upon providing your advice, notice how the patient absorbs or interprets your message. This may affect your treatment efficacy. Messaging should be clear and concise and not populated with jargon. All industry groups use jargon, and this can be jarring for the patient to hear. Your messaging should be in plain language that they will understand and absorb. Your messaging should be relevant to their problem. Examples from other treatments you may have provided may be useful, but personalise the message to their problem.

Deliver your advice carefully. The best way for you to provide your advice is to make sure you do not bombard the patient with too much of it. I suggest two or three clear pieces of advice is enough.

Reflecting empathy is a wonderful way for the patient to be sure that you actively listened. For example, if the patient advised that their injury/condition is making it difficult for them to study or work, then simply reply with a statement, such as: "I understand that your problem is making your work life difficult, and you feel you are not able to be productive." The key words here are the empathetic words *understand* and *feel*.

Therapy

The therapy you apply may be mobilising or manipulation, advice, counselling, prescriptive instructions, or involve detail of what the patient may need to do at home. Alternatively, therapy may be the provision of a clear diagnosis and patient reassurance.

If you are counselling the patient, you may have developed a plan with them about how to manage their currently overwhelming problem by breaking their problem down to smaller-to-deal-with bites. Start with something easy and manageable like suggesting they compile some notes in a diary, or they speak with a close family member or colleague. How you manage the patient interaction — be it with manual therapy, by empathetic concern in your words, treatment progressions or plan development — is crucial to gain trust and to ensure the patient will be compliant with the therapy. If you are a manual therapist, then practise these skills to ensure confident and competent handling.

Exercise and advice progression are also key elements of clinical reasoning. Progression of a patient's treatment will ensure that they improve. Doing the same thing each visit without progression is a sure way for your patient to seek treatment elsewhere.

Improving your clinical reasoning will allow you to understand how to best progress treatment for a patient who has an acute problem. Carefully base your therapy on the extent of the injury/pathology. Therapy with a more chronic condition involves slower expectations of efficacy, but the treatment may be progressed more quickly, or the therapy be administered more intensely, depending on what is applicable at a particular stage of your clinical reasoning. Good clinical reasoning will assist compliance with application of treatment/therapy when the patient is not with you, be that by the use of ice, heat, massage crème, exercises, relaxation techniques and medications.

Actions and Behaviours

Reassessing your patient's condition after the application of therapy is essential. Using a model where you apply an intervention and then reassess the reaction to the intervention will develop your clinical reasoning and assist with knowing the efficacy of the therapy. If the patient suggests they are worse after a treatment, this is not necessarily bad. In some cases this might mean you are on the right track and can adjust what you do from then on to compensate. Adjusting your clinical behaviours when treating a patient will also build confidence and trust.

To ensure a more complete recovery, try to achieve patient compliance with your directives and treatment. Demonstrating your competence and clinical skills will be a part of this. The patient can negatively interpret overconfidence, so it is best to under-promise and over-deliver.

Developing good clinical behaviours will assist you with your patient interactions. Simple things like providing a glass of water on a sweltering day, getting another pillow for comfort, having a quiet space to work in are such behaviours. Your own progress as a clinician will develop as your reasoning develops. Provide clear instructions to ensure the patient fully understands that to progress they must address their home exercise or the other activities you have prescribed. Make them aware of the downside of not complying. Knowing the timeframe and milestones to recovery are also elements that will ensure they progress as you intend and wish.

1.2.3 Training Processes

I have broken training down under five key headings: Clinical Mentors, Personal and Professional Development, Observation, Courses, and Volunteering.

Clinical Mentors

Having a clinical mentor will assist you to progress your clinical practice. The process of identifying the best clinical mentor for you is not always easy to do. If you are working in a practice with a principal or with others, this is a good place to start the identification process. Suitable mentors should be those who have strong, busy patient lists, who lecture or conduct courses publicly, who are available and have a desire to teach others. Quite a list!

Have your mentor first assess the level of your clinical ability to ensure their teaching fits your current abilities. This process needs to be formal and scheduled. I have found that most good practitioners have a passion for teaching and sharing their knowledge and abilities. So start your search at the practice you work at. Ask your peers if they know someone who may suit your needs. Be bold and do not be afraid to ask. Your mentoring can be one-to-one or one-to-many. Sometimes learning in a group facilitates better learning, but be aware that the progress of the group develops at the pace of the group's least able member and may not suit you.

At the networks I have operated and worked in,

we identified a practitioner who met the capabilities mentioned in the list above and every month this practitioner would conduct what we called "new and younger grad mentoring". The focus was on clinical reasoning and manual handling. The younger grads stayed in this group for two years.

Personal and Professional Development

There are other actions you can take to improve your abilities. Reading at least two to four relevant articles per month is important to ensure you are up to date in clinical practice. Similarly, listening to podcasts is an effective method of learning. I recommend that you try and achieve five to six hours per month of such learning.

Observation

This can be a part of your mentor's teaching or can be extremely specific with a certain practitioner who conducts a practice that has a particular focus. For example, the practitioner might treat many patients with headaches or patients experiencing back pain, or tendon injuries and so on. You may be surprised how willing experienced people can be in availing of their time to do such teaching. Try to achieve formal observations twice a month for two hours per observation.

Courses

In your early years as a practitioner there will be opportunities to attend available courses. The practice you work in may offer courses for their practitioners as well. I recommend that you do general courses rather than those with a narrow focus. A good example would be to do a shoulder course or a dealing-with-difficult-people workshop rather than something more esoteric that you may not see in practice very often, for example, post-fracture or post-surgical rehabilitation. Set your focus on problems and conditions that commonly present in your practice. Courses that develop your skills with such everyday problems should be the focus in this first stage.

Volunteering

Making yourself available to volunteer at all stages of your career is extremely rewarding. In your early career, working at a local sporting club free of charge, for example, will assist your learning and start to build your reputation and progression to clinical excellence. Developing better skills with this type of work experience will also build your patient list over time and provide a profound sense of satisfaction and belonging in your community.

1.2.4 Time Management and Planning

Most undergraduate programs in healthcare do not focus on planning. Undergraduate training will help you to structure your consultation and treatments, but not assist you with how you manage your time or perform other important activities and tasks, such as attending courses or reading articles. Detailed and effective planning involves making efficient use of your time. Sometimes it is called 'time management' or 'time leadership'. Effective time management will assist your productivity and focus. In his book *The Seven Habits of Highly Effective People*, Steven Covey uses a model that he named the 'Time Management Matrix'. I have found this model best captures the challenges and benefits of effective time management, see below.

Time Management Matrix

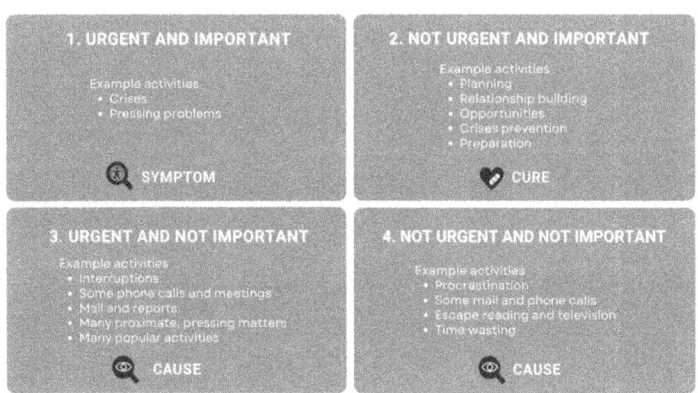

Figure 4: Time Management Matrix

This matrix applies to your activities at any point in your career. The quadrant where your time is both 'not urgent and important' (top right) is the quadrant in which you should strive to spend most of your time. Developing a strategy to ensure you spend your time in that quadrant is important. Understanding how to plan for important but non-urgent activities/actions will be covered in Stage Two of this book.

Urgent tasks as described in the left half of the table can be either important or not important, but you are not always going to know how important a phone call might be and therefore that call needs to be answered. Similarly, spending all your time in a quadrant where the activity is both unimportant and not urgent can be a distraction and a time waster. Social media can be pleasurable and help you connect with others effectively but can also be non-productive at other times.

In your journey focusing on making time available to plan, to develop relationships and prepare will see you make better use of the available time you have. Better use of time will improve your productivity and help you learn.

1.2.5 Goal Setting

Most undergraduate programs do not focus on setting and recording goals. I find that setting goals is fundamental to increasing your chances of achieving them. A theme for this book is to make sure your goals are Specific, Measurable, Achievable, Realistic and Timely — otherwise known as SMART goals.

Research supports the advantages of goal setting. For

example, a study into goal setting conducted in 2007 by Dr Gail Matthews, a psychology professor at the Dominican University of California, provides clear evidence that those who write down their goals accomplish significantly more than those who do not write their goals. I particularly like this study because its goal-setting group 'number five' responded with a document very similar to my Achieving Your Career Objectives document, which I have provided in Appendix 1. (Great minds think alike!)

In my practice networks working with clinicians, I created a simple approach to setting goals. My approach was firstly to create a clear goal, e.g. to improve my exercise prescription for lower limb injuries. The second step was to determine three methods for achieving this goal:

- Watch a practitioner deliver a program of exercises for a lower limb injury.

- Read an article about exercise prescription.

- Attend a course where the topic is directed to lower limb injury treatment.

The third step was to determine a Key Performance Indicator (KPI) for each method that would ensure I applied myself in a timely and thorough way:

- Watch an experienced practitioner for three sessions of four hours in the following month.

- Read three articles in the next month.

- Attend a relevant course in the next six months.

Note that the above goals have a clear action and a clearly defined timeline and have a binary outcome. You can say either yes or no if the actions were achieved.

The above is an example of a quantitative goal that you can apply in order to respond with either: yes, I achieved that goal; or no, I did not. Not all goals are quantitative. Some are qualitative. Qualitative goals are also important and the plan should contain some of these goals. For example, the goal might be: to feel more a part of the team over the next six months. How will you measure this goal 'to feel'? Even though it is not easy to measure the outcome of this goal, it is important to write it down so that in six months you can ask yourself whether you feel more a part of the team. Colleagues can also be asked if they think you are indeed now more a part of the team.

To help with the above, we developed a document in my network called Achieving Your Career Objectives (see Appendix 1).

This document directed clinicians to cover goals in five main aspects:

1. **Clinical** — the document outlines some goals and actions that will assist you to be more clinically excellent.

2. **Commercial and revenue generation** — this outlines the goals you need to develop commercially so you can observe how you improve or not over time.

3. **Risk management** — don't be surprised that at times a practitioner may not complete their notes or remember to renew insurances or their registration. Focusing on these matters is good to reduce risks, e.g. contracts, complaints, OH&S, work/life balance.

4. **Administration** — attending to the important aspects of your practice and personal development involves planning and administration, e.g. completing referrer tracker, service standards, compensable body paperwork.

5. **Research/postgraduate** — as part of developing your career, further education and possible involvement in research should be a focus and hence goals need to be set for these activities.

Once your goals are set, feedback on your level of performance against them in the period under review should be completed by your mentor. Mentors can also assist with setting realistic and achievable goals. Make sure the goals are also timely, fit for purpose and will enable you the satisfaction of achieving them.

As you progress on your career journey, your goals will change and develop in depth, relevance, detail, complexity and quality. At each stage of your journey setting goals should be a key function of your planning.

1.2.6 Effectiveness and Efficiency

Being effective is based on how you work with people, how you develop relationships and work towards a coherent plan and progress through your career. Efficiency is the way you get things done. Being efficient relates more to actual things that need to be done and usually do not involve relationships. For example, if you do not efficiently arrange a meeting time with your mentor, then you will not be able to have an effective engagement with them. By applying yourself to understanding these behaviours and then seeking feedback from others about how you are performing, you will gradually learn how to be more effective and efficient.

I created the following model to emphasise and clarify the differences between these two useful modes of working.

The Communication Model

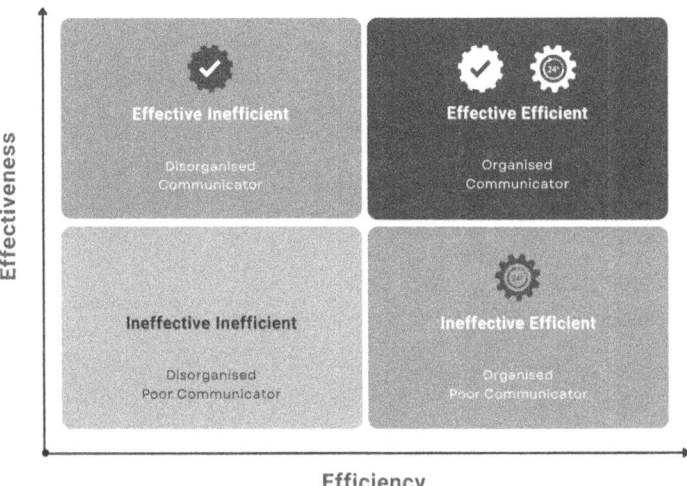

Figure 5: The Communication Model

I think we've all worked with people who occupy each of these quadrants. The people we have worked best with are in the top right quadrant. As such, you should always strive for that quadrant of the model: being an organised communicator. You will occupy different quadrants at certain times, so don't despair if you drift into moments of being ineffective and inefficient, as long as you are aware of this and are striving for the top right. A good example is that you could take two hours treating a patient when that patient only required a thirty-minute treatment. This is an inefficient use of time and that extra hour-and-a-half spent doesn't necessarily lead to an effective treatment outcome.

1.2.7 Essential Behaviours

When you commence your practice, you will not always be busy with patient treatment. With input from many effective and efficient practitioners, I've condensed some essential behaviours that all practitioners should aspire to. These behaviours can be summarised under three headings: The Essential Activities of an Effective Practitioner, What To Do When You Are Not Busy, and Relationship Marketing.

The Essential Activities of an Effective Practitioner

1. Never Turn a Patient Away

People who are coming to see you are often making a distress purchase. Even if we don't necessarily believe that it's vital their condition is treated immediately, the patient may want and expect this. If they don't get in to see you, they will often call someone else who can help them. It may be difficult to attend to another patient when you already have people booked in and you don't want to compromise the care of the patient by making the appointment while you are already busy. A few suggestions are:

- Explain to the new patient directly or via reception that you're very busy but will do everything you can to help. This may decrease their expectations a little, which is only fair given your situation. Explain you may have to decrease the normal time you spend with them, but that will not compromise the quality you can provide.

- Explain to your patients with appointments there has been an emergency and apologise for any inconvenience this will cause them.

- Check your patient list to see if there are any patients coming in soon who you know would be comfortable seeing one of the other practitioners working with you.

- If you have a future gap in your list, try calling your other patients to see if one can reschedule.

- If you are running late, call your other patients to let them know — just as a courtesy.

2. See Your New Patients the Next Day

For a moment, pretend you are Cathy Freeman's practitioner and it is the week before the 2000 Sydney Olympics where she aims to win gold in the 400 metres.

Cathy comes to you with an injury. You may not think it is a serious injury, but Cathy is concerned enough to have come in to see you. Regardless of the injury, when would you suggest she comes back to see you again? If you are trying to provide the highest quality care, the answer is tomorrow — at the latest! Yet as a profession, we seem to be in the habit of telling people to come back in two or three days, perhaps a week. There may be the occasional circumstance where it may not be appropriate or practical to see your new patient the next day, but if you are trying to offer the highest quality care this is likely to be infrequent. Your patient will advise you if a next-day appointment does not suit them, but they will not do this if they are not first asked to attend the next day.

3. Count and Measure What You Do

In clinical practice we like to measure and re-measure the results of any intervention. We try to be objective. If we measure and remain objective, it makes it easier to help our patients. It's the same with measuring patient numbers, revenues and other progress. Obtain baseline measurements, set some goals, work towards your goals, re-measure and adjust as necessary. We often spend too much time with our heads down doing our treatments and not enough time analysing whether we're really offering patients what they want and need. Counting and measuring is a vital start in this process.

4. Thank Your Referrers

It may be a letter regarding each patient, it may be a Christmas card, it may be taking them for a game of golf. Don't assume that if someone is referring now, they will keep referring. The way to maintain them as a referrer is by regular communication and acknowledgement.

5. Transfer Trust

There will be times when you are on holidays, away with a team, unwell or unavailable, and the patient list you have worked so hard to develop can seem to disappear. To minimise the drop-off rate, you need to successfully transfer the trust you have developed with your patients, across to other practitioners within your practice. Likewise, your other practitioners need to transfer the trust of their patients across to you when they are unavailable. How is this done? Educate your patients by informing them you may be unavailable, reinforce the positive qualities of the other practitioners, try to introduce your patient to the other practitioner you are suggesting that your patient could see before you become unavailable, and reassure the patient all their necessary history and treatment details are in your notes.

6. Be on Time

Patients will have increasing expectations of your service. They expect to be seen very close to their appointment time.

They expect not to have their appointments changed often. They expect their practitioner to be available to them.

7. Set Patient Expectations

Some patients may simply expect too much from their visit. You need to educate them so they have realistic expectations. For example, by saying: "Your pain may increase a little after treatment, but this is normal and nothing to worry about. It's part of the process to recovery and the pain should diminish soon after your treatment."

8. Change the Patient

Never let a patient leave feeling the same as when they came in. For example, even if you don't think you have identified a clear diagnosis, you should attempt to educate them about the possible differential diagnoses or get them to ride a bike or do some activities that may elicit more information about their diagnosis. You can then reassess to ascertain if their pain/condition has changed or otherwise. Even if they are worse after the consult, by clarifying their expectation this can be a positive. If your patient leaves the consult thinking that you have assisted them, either by informing them, educating them, or even referring them to another practitioner with more experience, then they will not perceive the consult as a waste of time. Never try and bluff a patient that you know something when you do not.

Underlying all of these suggestions are three fundamental concepts:

- Do unto others as you would have them do unto you.

- We aim to exceed expectations, not just meet them.

- Remember that you are often judged more on your non-clinical skills.

What To Do When You Are Not Busy

The important things to do when you have spare time are usually the hardest. Just like the adage that says you only realise your room needs cleaning when you have to sit down to study, a similar form of procrastination can occur when it comes to promoting your practice. The most important thing to do when you are not busy is to build up your patient list to make yourself busier. The problem for practitioners is that spare time usually occurs in small increments. It is common to have 15 minutes here and 30 minutes there. This makes it difficult to be effective with such a short amount of time. However, the professionals who use that time most effectively are usually the most successful.

When teaching time management, I sometimes help practitioners to understand and remember with the following example: you have a glass jar, some rocks, sand and water. The jar represents the time you have in a day.

The rocks are the big important things to do, and the grains of sand are the regular things to do in your day. The water represents your very small activities. If you fill the jar with sand first, you can't fit many rocks in. But if you fill the jar with rocks, then it is easy to fill the spaces left with sand and then fill the jar with water at the end. Do the important tasks first because you will always have little tasks to do. Here's a list of things to do when you are not busy to help you build up your patient list:

1. Ensure Your Current Patients Receive Excellent Service

Current patients are ultimately the greatest source of referrals to you. The extra five minutes you spend discussing their son's sore foot, or creating a personalised exercise sheet, or writing a letter to their coach are examples that will assist you to exceed their expectations.

2. Ring a Client

Ring a client who has been discharged, or has not attended for an appointment, and enquire about their progress. Ask if they are improving, if they are doing their exercises, and so on. Do not in any way pressure them, or tell them to attend for an appointment, as this makes you look like a salesperson, but communicate with true concern about how they are. Clients are always pleasantly surprised when a professional person calls them to ask how they are.

3. Thank, Ring or Visit a Referrer

Ensure each new patient has a letter from their referrer each and every time on DAY ONE.

Ringing a referrer may depend on the referrer's preferences, but in general a call is quicker and more effective than an email or a letter. Visiting a referrer can be possible if you have time. It may be better to jump in the car, get to your local doctor's office, pop your head in and ask if you can just say a quick hello. If the doctor is busy, leave some cards/referral pads/an article of interest with the receptionist. (Remember that sometimes the receptionist or practice manager is the most important person to develop a rapport with because they are often the gatekeeper for the doctor's clinic.)

4. Visit a Sports Club/Trainer

If you finish early on any given night, don't just think: "Great, I'll get home quicker." Use this time to visit your local sports team or trainer. If you can spend 15 to 30 minutes looking at injuries or talking to the trainer, or demonstrating a new strapping technique, then your input will be greatly valued by the club and trainer, and they will be far more likely to refer their players to you.

5. Tidy Up

Patients may judge you more by how neat and tidy the cubicle is than your knowledge. If you have five minutes before your next patient arrives, quickly check the cubicle, tidy the supply trolley(s), neaten any reading materials/articles, fold the towels, and so on. Act as if you are having guests come to your house.

6. Ring an Employer

Ring a worker's compensation case manager or business employer to let them know what success you are having with one of their employees that you are treating. They want to know when they may be back at work, what they will be able to do, and so on. They will also get the feeling you are really doing your best to get their people fixed! This may encourage them to send more people to visit you.

7. Review Your Patients' Treatment Plans

It is easy to forget when you are treating patients, especially those with lower back or complex problems, what other forms of treatment they may benefit from. Review your list and ask: "Should this person be in a group class, or a hydrotherapy program, or seeing a podiatrist, or ...?"

8. Catch Up

If you only have a few minutes or indeed seconds before your next patient, try to avoid wasting time with idle chat. You can finish a client's notes in this time, or review your list, or check the waiting room to see if someone is early, and so on. All of these activities allow you to be more prepared if the unexpected happens. If a new person walks in the door in pain, you will have those extra few minutes up your sleeve that can make the difference between being able to see them or being overly rushed. Ideally, you should never be too busy to take action to catch up. Catching up is a good thing and will help you build your patient list. Using your time effectively will also help and is a valuable skill to develop. It takes practice and discipline, but it is worth the effort.

Relationship Marketing

Relationship marketing refers to activities that focus on communication and other behaviours that help to grow and develop relationships via your existing patients and referrers. Why is this so important? Ask yourself the following questions: Where do my patients come from? Do they attend my centre or book an appointment with me because they saw my building sign or looked up the internet? Are they likely to have been referred to me by an existing patient, from someone I know or from another health professional?

The basic fact is that the majority of patients attend your centre through referral by an existing patient or someone who knows you. The adage "The patient you see today is the source of your wealth tomorrow" still holds true. Relationship marketing is a growth strategy that creates advocates for your business. It is also a risk management strategy to prevent negativity around your business.

The diagram below describes the status of an individual's relationship with you as a healthcare practitioner. The aim is to help people progress up the Ladder of Loyalty. Progress up the ladder is driven by the development of a relationship with that patient.

The Ladder of Loyalty

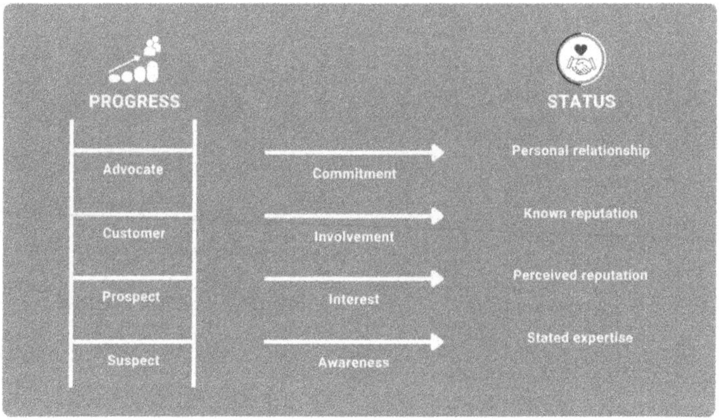

Figure 6: The Ladder of Loyalty

The four levels in the above diagram of your patient's progression from being a suspect to becoming an advocate can be explained as follows.

Level 1:   Suspect

At the first stage of involvement, the suspect is aware of your service, but no trigger points have been activated to stimulate their interest. These trigger points include advertising and promotions, public relations and personal interactions which make the 'suspect' aware of your expertise.

Level 2:   Prospect

The suspect (awareness) progresses to prospect (interest) as a consequence of a perceived need that is often reinforced by a referral or recommendation from a valued source. This recommendation elevates their perception of your reputation.

Level 3:   Customer

Prospect (interest) leads to Customer (action). Interactions with you will create first-party perception of your skills, knowledge and attributes. If all goes well, your actions will enhance your reputation and you will start to generate a relationship from which loyalty will flow.

Level 4:   Advocate

The customer relationship has developed to advocacy. Clear loyalty and respect are now inherent within the relationship. The customer becomes an advocate for your services and actively promotes you by word-of-mouth, generating potential new customers.

Let's go into more detail here about progressing a customer up the ladder to become an advocate. The old adage of ensuring your "Availability, Affability and Ability" still applies. However, my discussions with practitioners and from my experience highlight four other areas:

- Your professionalism — how you look, what you say, how you say it and deliver on your promises.

- Personalisation of your service — addressing their unique needs.

- Whether people engage with you — because you demonstrate real interest in them.

- Communication — the fundamental mechanism for developing relationships, especially empathy. Empathetic listening ensures you truly understand what your patient is saying and how they feel. This is vitally important.

1.3 Why is Clinical Excellence Important?

I think being clinically excellent is the key to your journey as a healthcare practitioner. If you have developed clinical excellence, then you are more likely to assist your clients with their health care needs.

There are a few other reasons why clinical excellence is important:

Learning

When you develop skills and eventually some mastery of your craft, then the process of learning becomes an enjoyable and iterative path that never reaches an end point. As your career develops, you continue learning and your thirst for learning will become insatiable.

Satisfaction

Producing better and better outcomes for your patients will provide you with a great sense of satisfaction and provides your community with better health and quality of life. Having a sense of pride in what you do is uplifting and will propel you continually forward in your career growth.

Building Your List

Seeing your list of patients grow will improve your earning capacity and assist you to meet your lifestyle needs. Clinical excellence is the pathway and gaining this early in your career is important when your passion for learning is high. Developing good habits early in your career will assist with future career progression.

Credibility

Good results with your treatments will build your credibility as a practitioner. This will result in more referrals and opportunities for you. Examples of such opportunities may be elite team involvement, requests to lecture, requests to assist more experienced practitioners with courses, and so on.

Career Progression

Increasing your clinical excellence will take you to the next level in your career. Next-level clinically excellent practitioners have higher demand for their services and will see more complex and challenging patients, which further develops their skills and abilities.

Operating Your Own Practice

The key to starting your own practice or taking equity in a practice, if that opportunity eventuates, will be enhanced if you have a strong clinical ability and can get results with the patients that you treat.

1.4 What Else Do I Need to Achieve Clinical Excellence?

In this chapter we have identified the need to be clinically excellent as part of the process of building your patient list. We have explored the key elements required to develop your clinical excellence and developed a pathway for you towards clinical excellence. I'm now going to outline some further factors that will assist you to achieve clinical excellence under the three main headings: Working in an Empowered Work Environment, Understanding the

Importance of the Three A's, and Developing a Unique Selling Proposition (USP).

1.4.1 Working in an Empowered Work Environment

An empowered work environment is a place where you have all you need to grow and develop. I will outline the extrinsic and intrinsic factors that identify if the environment you work in is such an environment.

A. The Extrinsic Factors:

Resources

When you are working in your practice, you need to have some resources to assist you. Having the right equipment is essential, e.g. access to files, access to the latest devices and methods used for treatments, such as specific equipment, heat, ice and other relevant materials. The work setting is also a resource for you. Comfortable seating, plinths, good lighting and a quiet space to work will add to the efficacy and effectiveness of your consult and treatment.

Managers/Mentors

I have mentioned the importance of mentors already. A good manager and good administration will help to streamline the visit of your patient and assist them to be relaxed and ready for the consult with you. A peer or trusted colleague to talk with about progress can help with reducing any nervousness you may have, particularly when you first commence consulting.

Being Trustworthy and Developing Trust

Establishing a trusting relationship, be it with peers or with your patient, is a foundation to successful communication, engagement and practice. Being trustworthy is a trait that will lead people to want to be with you, listen to you and this will assist your effectiveness. Being honest, meeting commitments, doing what you say you are going to do are all elements of trustworthiness.

Time and Patience

Taking time and being patient are difficult to navigate in the world we live in. People want things to happen and to see results now. In this book I will reference the work of Stephen Covey several times. His book *The Seven Habits of Effective People* was a pivotal text for me when I read it many years ago. I was fortunate enough to attend two workshops personally delivered by Dr Covey, where I was able to explore his concepts and ask questions directly to him. He sadly passed away when he had a bike-riding accident and is survived by his children, one of whom has continued his work. His book is still a bestseller. In *The Seven Habits of Highly Effective People*, Covey refers to "the law of the farm", which illustrates why time and patience are necessary.

Simply, this means sowing your crop in the autumn and harvesting in the spring. To sow the crop, you need to prepare the soil, fertilise the plants, remove weeds, apply water, and so on, to make sure the crop that you harvest is the best it can be. This takes time and patience.

Opportunities for Learning and Growth

In your empowered practice environment there will be times when you want to contribute with your ideas and this opportunity should hopefully be available to you. Training and teaching should also be a part of your practice. If these elements are not available, then you should ask why and offer to assist so that they are incorporated into the practice.

Challenging and Interesting Work

If the work you do is varied and challenges you, then you will grow your skills and abilities. This will not happen by chance, and in an empowered environment this type of work should be available for you. Do not hesitate to ask and keep asking for what you need to grow and develop.

B. The Intrinsic Factors:

Being Engaged and Enthusiastic

In the earlier Engagement Model (Figure 2) we investigated the idea of the intrinsic traits you can develop and show in your practice. There is no room for apathy in an empowered work environment.

Hard Work and Persistence

It is not necessarily bad to cruise along in your job, but in the longer term this will hold you back from opportunities that can come your way. If you are having difficulty and feel you are not progressing in your work, then make sure you persist, as you are often closer to breaking through the problem than you may think.

Express Your Personality and Individuality

People will connect with you if you let your personal traits and personality shine through. Developing your own practice style which is welcoming, enthusiastic, sincere and consistent will draw patients towards you.

1.4.2 Understanding the Importance of the Three A's

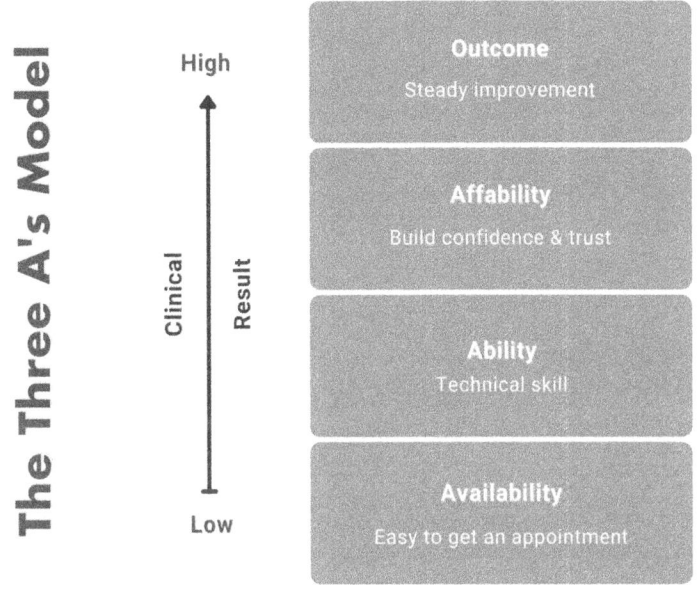

Figure 7: The Three A's Model

Availability

The best place to start is to make sure you are available to see your patients. This means making sure you are available most days and at times when your patients need to see you based on their schedules. If you have limited availability, you will not be able to build your client list.

Ability

Patients might not have the expertise to assess your technical ability. The only measure they will have will be whether they improve or not. If they improve, they will most likely attribute their improvement to your ability as a therapist. Continuing to improve your techniques, your knowledge of the conditions you treat and by constantly striving to learn, your competence and ability as a therapist will improve and your patient list will grow.

Affability

Affability (being friendly, sociable, jovial and gregarious) is a personal quality that in healthcare we all have to some degree. We are mostly drawn to such professions because we want to help others to live more fulfilling lives. Being more affable may be challenging as it implies that you need to work on your own nature. Some people are natural extroverts and find it easy to develop rapport and to influence people. I am not suggesting that if you are an introvert that you cannot be affable. Kindness and caring are recognised by patients and if you sincerely work on displaying such traits, then you will achieve the outcomes you and your patients desire.

Outcome

Each of these elements will contribute to the outcome of your interaction with the patient. I believe you need all three to succeed. Put simply: if you have Ability, then you have the fundamental tools, techniques and know-how to provide the best possible treatment; if you have Availability, then you will have appointment times that suit your patients' lifestyles; if you have Affability, then you can connect well with your patients so they listen to you and are therefore more likely to follow your advice and instructions that will contribute to their improvement. In summary, you will then have the Three A's working together to achieve the best possible outcome for your patients.

When you commence your practice, you may only have two of the Three A's in place — Availability and Affability — but working to improve your Abilities will provide a clear pathway for you to improve and develop your treatments and consequently grow your patient list.

1.4.3 Developing a Unique Selling Proposition (USP)

It is never too early to start exploring your interests. You will be drawn to certain people, and particular conditions, injuries, diagnoses and problems your patients may present with.

A patient list will often grow with patients whom you have a rapport with, whom you develop a liking for, and patients who are maybe a little like you in age, interests and temperament. We can call such patients the 'ideal patients' for you. In addition to the personal traits of a patient, you will find that certain injury or problem presentations provide the most satisfaction for you to treat. If you develop this satisfaction, then you will see more of these conditions and be continually improving your skills with these conditions. When this happens, you are developing a Unique Selling Proposition (USP).

A USP will become a marketing tool for you when you speak with potential referrers, and your patients will use this to tell others about how you are uniquely able to assist them. We will cover the important issue of a USP in more detail as we explore how you work towards commercial success in the next stage of your journey.

Clinical excellence is something that will be part of your practice for your entire clinical journey. This is the cornerstone of how you develop commercial success. In Stage Two I will explore how to apply your clinical excellence in a commercial way to develop your career.

2.0 STAGE TWO

Owning Your List — Commercial Success

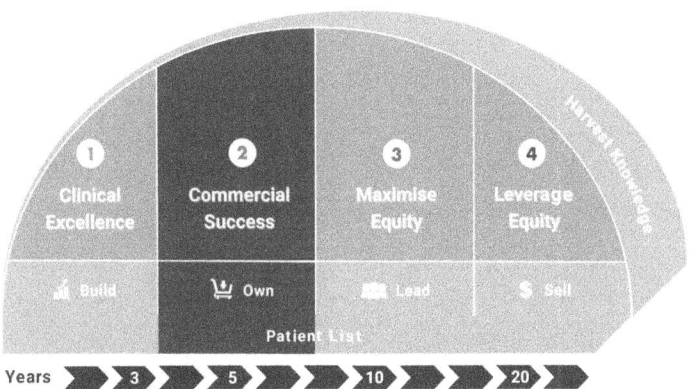

In Stage Two we explore how to apply your clinical excellence in a commercial way to develop your career. Clinical excellence is ongoing throughout your journey. But at the end of Stage One I define clinical excellence in practitioner terms, namely a practitioner who is achieving good outcomes with their patient treatments, i.e. you are treating patients well and getting good results. There will also be an increasing confidence in your ability during this first stage and you will feel ready to treat more patients and earn more income.

The next stage for you is what I will call 'commercial success'. In this second stage you will build a full list of patients and then move to owning this list. What 'owning your list' means is the patients you see become accustomed to seeing you, recommend you to others, and generally prefer to see you over any other practitioner in your discipline. If you go on annual leave, for instance, they will see others but will likely revert to seeing you when you return from annual leave. If you leave the practice, then these patients will possibly seek you out, i.e. they will follow you. At the end of Stage Two, you will have a full list that you own and you will therefore have achieved commercial success.

2.1 Who is Stage Two For?

Your journey is a process of building skills that see your career progress. The important stage of acquiring clinical excellence never ceases, as you can always improve your skills, knowledge and abilities. That said, you can now focus on how you might grow your list further and consolidate your financial situation and growing expertise.

This stage is for those who have developed: Clinical Excellence, A Desire to Earn More Money, A Want to Develop and Grow Your USP, and Have Experience Three to Five Years Post-Graduation.

Clinical Excellence

Up to this point you have been developing your clinical excellence. I will keep re-emphasising this throughout your entire practitioner journey. If you or your mentors/supervisors are unsure that you have reached this point, then moving to Stage Two should be delayed until you and they are confident in your skills and abilities.

A Desire to Earn More Money

Up until now your focus has not been directed to the income you are generating, but on improving your clinical practice. Once you're on your way to clinical excellence, you have earned the opportunity to look at what will make you commercially successful. Growing your income will come from seeing more patients, of course, but it will also come by being more productive with your time and more effective with your treatments.

A Want to Develop and Grow Your Unique Selling Proposition (USP)

In Stage One we talked a little about identifying a USP. What you like doing and what you consider your strength enables you to focus on how you can see more patients with certain conditions you know well and can progress to full recovery. Examples of USPs are: an interest and expertise in treating migraine headaches or a special interest in chronic lower back pain or a high level of confidence in treating tendon injuries, and so on. Developing that USP takes time and extra learning, so that you may eventually be known as the practitioner with that certain skill who attracts a wider range of referrers and creates the opportunity to market those strengths (your USP) to referrers.

Have Experience Three to Five Years Post-Graduation

The timelines I create are somewhat arbitrary. You may reach them sooner or take longer, hence the range. If you have applied yourself well to the first stage of this book, then you are ready to take action and plan how you will now become commercially successful.

2.2 What is Commercial Success?

To become commercially successful, you will need to address four major activities:

1. Development of a full list.

2. Strategies to own your list.

3. Being able to measure your success by the development and achievement of key performance indicators, i.e. measurement.

4. Having a clear, objective, achievable plan that you follow that keeps you focused and on track, i.e. a marketing plan.

2.2.1 Development of a Full List

So what do I mean by a full list? A full list of patients means that on any given day you are 80-90% booked. It is difficult to be 100% booked all the time because some patients may ring and cancel as they are sick, some may forget and not turn up, or some may decide that they do not wish to continue treatment for a variety of reasons. Do not be perturbed by this, and make sure that you investigate why people cancel. This can be done by asking reception staff to advise you when patients do cancel and to find out if they rebook. I did a short survey at one of our practices and identified that roughly 12% of patients change their appointment for some reason. If this is your rate of patient changes, then consider it normal.

A full list also means you are earning more income as the numbers of patients you see grows, providing you with greater satisfaction and greater personal spending power. There are four major things that will help you to achieve full list: Experience and Handling, More Referrers, Credibility with Others, and becoming the Practitioner of Choice.

Experience and Handling

As you treat more patients, your experience and handling of the patient consult will improve and you will become more adept at identifying signs of any lack of progress, lagging patient compliance or disaffection with the level of satisfaction your treatment is providing. This enables you to change course if you need to before the patient may become disengaged or disgruntled with progress. An example of this disengagement will be lack of compliance with direction, missing appointments or suggestions from your patient that they are keen to seek another opinion about their condition and progress. Alternatively, if your patient is happy with your experience and handling, they will speak highly of you and recommend you to others.

More Referrers

More referrers will help you to achieve a full list. Be sure to continue asking each and every new patient how they came to see you. You need to identify whether they were directed to you by referral or by word-of-mouth or if they came to the practice before to see someone else, or they found the practice through the myriad of possible digital channels. I have always encouraged practitioners to collect this information and even record this information in a referrer tracker. Such a document can take many forms, but I suggest you keep the detail under headings:

- Name of referrer or source
- Word-of-mouth (if so referred)
- Date they attended
- The injury or condition
- Contact details

Credibility with Others

It may sound strange, but the more patients you see the more the credibility among your peers and the staff you work with grows. It's a snowball effect. As your list grows, it will accelerate. If you experience this then that's a sure sign that you're approaching a full list. Credibility creates opportunities to talk about your practice, to start to deliver academic papers, or to be able to apply for positions in sports or other teams, or have offers to work different practices you may wish to work at.

Practitioner of Choice

Once you have a full list of patients, your patients will identify you as their practitioner of choice. These patients will seek you out wherever you are, even if you decide to leave your practice and work somewhere else, or start your own practice. On average, at this stage, at least 50% of your patients will follow you to another business or location. They will at least try to find you unless you move too far from the location where you were treating them. Retaining 50% of patients is a good outcome for you, but might become a two-edged sword once you're a business owner because you may have to deal with a loss of patients if one of your own practitioners leaves the practice.

2.2.2 Strategies to Own Your List

There are a number of strategies to execute on the path to owning your list. By steadily attending to the matters below you will notice that your patient list, which may have been patchy with a number of vacant appointments, will start to be more consistently booked.

These are the four strategies to achieve this:

1. Patient relationship building

2. Referrer relationship building

3. Ongoing development of clinical excellence

4. Developing your own personal brand

Patient Relationship Building

There are three key elements to patient relationship building: Emotional Bank Account, Circle of Influence, and Persuasion.

Emotional Bank Account

Having an easy rapport with patients will build your confidence and encourage patients to return to see you again should they suffer a subsequent injury or problem with their health. In Stephen Covey's book *The Seven Habits of Highly Effective People*, he speaks of developing a positive Emotional Bank Account (EBA) with your interactions in all aspects of your life. If we divide the relationships we have as either being in a positive, a neutral or a negative space, then if the space is neutral the EBA is considered to be at the base line. In other words, your bank account is neither in credit nor in debit. If you make deposits (a kind gesture, meeting a commitment, caring over and above what is expected, and so on) then the bank account will be in credit. Conversely, the account can easily drift into debit when you do not attend to the needs or desires of the relationship. If we continue to make these withdrawals/debits, then it becomes harder to get the bank account back into balance. In this case it is possible that many small deposits may be needed to get the balance back to credit and hence the relationship may be rocky while you do that. With patient interaction running late, or changing the appointment, or constantly leaving the room while you are treating them, and so forth, these are withdrawals from the EBA. Be aware of the importance of having a positive EBA in all your relationships.

The EBA Model

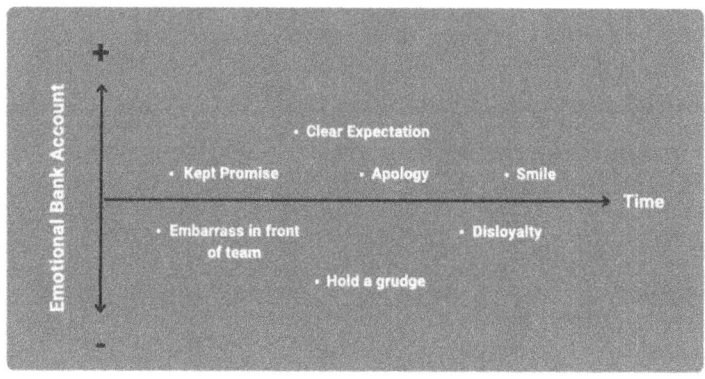

Figure 8: The EBA Model

There are certain customer service imperatives that you should strive to always attend to that help to develop a positive EBA. The three that are most important are:

- A warm and sincere greeting to patients will ensure that the consultation starts well. Make eye contact, don't turn your back to the patient and remember to smile.

- Personalisation of the service. This is demonstrated by remembering key details that patients may have told you about their family, or helping them get up from the chair. Such activity will endear you to the patient.

- A fond and caring farewell will leave your patient with a good memory of the experience they have just had with you.

It is important that such behaviours are also part of the experience your patient has with reception or admin staff, so don't let a bad experience like a mistake with billing, muddled appointment times or other matters interfere with your relationship with your patients. If you become aware that such actions are occurring, then make sure you speak with these staff or make the practice principal aware that such actions may be taking place.

Circle of Influence

Another lesson I have learnt from Stephen Covey's *Seven Habits of Highly Effective People* is to focus on your circle of influence, rather than your circle of concern. Applying this approach will help you focus on what you can truly change, not on activities outside your sphere of influence that you cannot control (like complaining about the weather!!)

The Circle of Influence

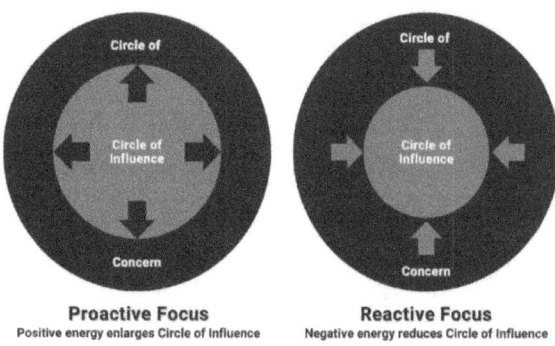

The Circle of Concern

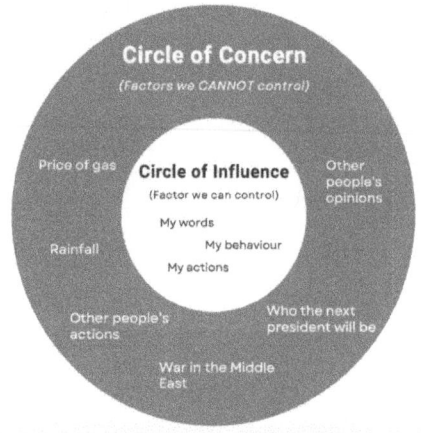

Figure 9: Circle of Influence and Circle of Concern*

The Circle of Concern is the larger outer circle, which

---

* The Circle of Influence and the Circle of Concern diagrams are reproduced from the book *The 7 Habits of Highly Successful People* by Stephen R. Covey (1990) and is reproduced with the permission of Simon & Schuster, US.

represents everything you care about. The Circle of Influence is the smaller inner circle and consists of everything you have direct control over. The larger your Circle of Concern is, the smaller your Circle of Influence becomes because you can only pay attention to a limited number of things at once. By focusing on your broader worries, you can end up having less control over what you want to achieve or can influence. By proactively working from your Circle of Influence, you will learn that you can achieve more and be less worried and stressed about the things that you cannot control.

Overall, I believe that we all have to develop self-leadership to ensure we focus on what we can influence, rather than be concerned about what we can't. Here are three important leadership traits to learn and develop:

- Continual learning and then teaching. Self-teaching shows leadership and the discipline to continue your learning will prepare you for teaching others. This is a key part of leadership in your journey.

- Good communication with others. Good leaders are good communicators. Work on developing the skill of positive, effective, and enthusiastic communication as this will assist you in developing referrers, building your list and working collaboratively in a practice.

- Making a coherent plan that you follow. Your plan is your secret to getting things done and becoming commercially successful. I will say this again because it is very important from my viewpoint: plan time to plan!

Persuasion

I once picked up a magazine in an airport lounge. In that magazine there was an article about a book by American psychologist Robert Cialdini titled *Influence: The Psychology of Persuasion*. In this book Cialdini explains how people can be persuaded and influenced in terms of six principles of social influence. I was fascinated how social science had developed a framework that demonstrated how we are all influenced by advertisements and by others. I think these principles can be applied to your practice and help you to influence others in order to be compliant with treatment and to encourage them to refer clients to you.

I will outline these six principles and their relevance to health practitioners:

1. Reciprocation (we feel obligated to return favours provided for us)

An example of how reciprocation can be applied is to think about a sports club that is near your practice that you wish to have the players at that club use your services. Using the principle of reciprocation you would attend training at that club on the next training day after the weekend game. Offer to assess the players' injuries and advise the club that you are happy to do this to build your relationship with this club. Without doing anything else, you will see that the players and the club will reciprocate by making appointments to visit you at your practice. I have done this at a club three kilometres from my practice and over time I gained four to five appointments every week. Eventually, I ceased going to the club but the referrals continued. After I ceased practising there, the club continued to refer to the practice.

2. Authority (we look to experts to show us the way)

When you visit a medical specialist, you might notice that the walls are adorned by qualifications. This indicates authority and is attempting to show you that the specialist is an authority who will assist you. You might use authority by framing and placing certificates from courses you have attended or wear a white coat with a name badge. Such things are not popular anymore and may create a formality that is a barrier, but they and other activities — such as discussing courses you have attended or articles you have read that are relevant to the patient's condition — can work to establish your authority.

3. **Commitment/Consistency (we want to act consistently with our commitments and in accordance with our values)**

Not everybody behaves in this way, but many of us strive to do so. Being committed and consistent builds confidence and trust in those we meet, work with, or treat as patients. We want our patients to say things like: "Michael always runs on time or calls if he is running late", "Jane consistently has increased her learning by attending workshops", and "Jack will always take time to speak with you or spend that little bit of extra time to assist." Such activities show commitment and consistency and will build your credibility and relevance to referrers and others.

4. **Scarcity (the less available the resource the more people want it).**

Have you ever needed to see a medical specialist or leader in their field? Often the appointment will not be in a few days (unless life-threatening) or even weeks. Such an appointment is valuable and scarce. You would never think under these circumstances to miss that appointment. This is the principle of scarcity. This can be used in the practice to build your list. Ask your admin staff to only offer a limited number of appointment options or, if online, do not give multiple options for people to book, as they will not place as much value on that appointment if they think they have many and multiple options.

5. **Liking (the more we like people the more we want to say yes)**

Sales people will always try to be pleasant and befriend you. They want you to like them. Being friendly and helpful will see people start to like you. Once they do, they will be happy to make appointments and return for visits. You don't have to overdo it. Basic friendliness, kindness and helpfulness will do the trick.

6. **Social proof (we look to what others do to guide our behaviour)**

Cialdini's book provides a great example to illustrate this principle. He details a park in the USA with a very old forest. Some of the trees are so old that pieces of the wood have become petrified. The park used to have sign that said: "This wood is very precious and there is a limited amount of it left. Please do not take the wood." They found that the signage accelerated the taking of the wood because people knew it was scarce (the scarcity principle). They then created a new sign. The sign said simply: "Most people who visit this park do not take the wood." With this new signage, the taking of the wood decreased by 90%. Most people tend to do what the majority do.

Think about this when you create a marketing campaign or new service. Using the sentence "We find that most people with back pain attend back education classes" will see more people likely to sign up for that class. Another example can often be seen in practices with a special interest in elite sport, where they will place signed photos on their walls of athletes performing at high-level events like the Olympics. This demonstrates the principle of social proof (and the principle of authority). Seeing this proof should encourage people to visit the practice, as it implies the elite also attend and hence the practice should be able to assist them too.

Referrer Relationship Building

The idea of building relationships with referrers may seem like a frightening activity for you to pursue. I call this Relationship Marketing. When presenting these ideas to younger practitioners I will often receive the reply: "I have not been trained in marketing." This may be true, although some allied health courses focus heavily on marketing because they realise that most of those who graduate will move into private practice and will need to know how to build a practice or a business. My response to "I have not been trained in marketing" is to ask questions relating to the building of their personal relationships. How do you go about nurturing friendships, for example? If you have friends, do you arrange times to catch up and then not show up? Are you rude and unhelpful when your friends ask for your help? Do you return their calls, remember their birthdays? And so on. Although this is a little bit different, applying the same principles will assist you in building relationships with referrers.

There are some important points about referrer relationship building that I will discuss under the following five headings: Benefits and Risks of Referring, Strategic Relationship Development, Gifts and Acknowledgement of Good Referrers, Made-to-Stick Messaging, and RMBD Strategies.

1. Benefits and Risks of Referring

There are both benefits and risks for someone to refer to you. You need to negate the risk and propagate the benefit.

Risk Benefit Reward Model

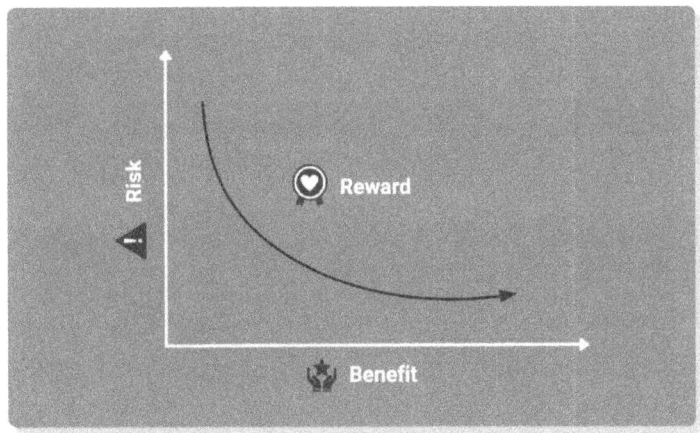

Figure 10: Risk-Benefit Reward Model

A. The Benefits to the Referrer

Be aware of the benefits you can provide to a referrer. Here is a list of benefits you might be able to provide:

Diagnosis/clinical reasoning

When you receive a referral, you have the opportunity to show your knowledge by assisting with a diagnosis to a problem, hence the referral. By using the reasoning skills you have developed, you can show how a complex problem can be addressed and highlight the progress made with the patient's condition or injury. When the patient meets the referrer again, they will advise positively about how your treatment helped them

Improved outcomes

As you receive more referrals, the outcomes of treatment should improve and, when you communicate this to the referrer, their opinion of you should be enhanced. This will help you to become their preferred clinician for referrals.

Increased status for the referrer

Your patient will view the primary clinician who has referred to you more positively and this will increase the status of the referrer.

Loyalty (reciprocal referrals)

You can demonstrate loyalty to the referrer by making a

reciprocal referral to them when you need to do so. Once a referrer knows that you reciprocate, they will view you as being loyal to them and may refer more patients to you.

Offer care planning
In Australia the government systems provide what is known as a care plan. Such a plan is created by a medical doctor when someone has a chronic health problem or long-term injury. When the doctor creates a care plan, the government will provide a rebate for many allied health services. If you are part of that doctor's referral base, they will be happy to have you work with them to care for such patients.

Support and friendship
In some instances, a referrer will get to know you as you interact with them working on the care of mutual patients. The referrer will see you are a supportive colleague or even a friend. I know of many examples where a clinician has developed a friendship where they play golf together or attend professional functions together. If such a friendship develops, this is a benefit to the referrer.

B. The Risks of Referring
You should look to address and mitigate these risks:

Referrer could be seen to lack knowledge
A referrer will sometimes refer a patient and request

treatment be commenced without making a clear diagnosis. This is quite common. You may assess that treatment is not advised and that the diagnosis may be more complicated and that to apply treatment will not assist the condition. If so, you need to carefully convey your thoughts to the referrer and supportively advise that you think further investigation might be required before you provide treatment. This is particularly true if the referrer makes a diagnosis that you do not agree with. By being diplomatic, the referrer will not be seen to have made an error, lack knowledge or not have thoroughly assessed the patient's condition.

Referrer may lose control of the patient
When a patient is formally referred to you, make sure you update the referrer regularly so that the referrer is in control. If you do not agree with the suggested approach to the treatment of the patient, let the referrer know and encourage them to agree to a change of approach. They will then feel in control of their patient's care management.

Loss of a patient
I have observed the situation where a referred patient is then referred to another clinician by the treating practitioner. This is a mistake, and the referrer may then lose the patient from their practice altogether. Be aware of this risk because when the referrer finds out they may stop further referrals altogether.

Loss of revenue

If a patient continues treatment with you and does not return to the referrer, this could result in loss of income for the referrer. Make sure you always advise the patient to return to the referrer unless the patient has advised you that they have decided not to return to the referrer.

Poor response to treatment

If the patient does not respond well to your treatment, the patient will not only judge you and cease to see you, they may view the referrer in a negative way. Mitigate this risk by always updating the referrer about progress, and be prepared to send the patient back to the referrer if the patient is not progressing after three to four treatments.

Negative association with your fees

Advising referrers of your fees is important. Otherwise, the patient may return to the referrer and advise that they thought your fees were too high for the treatment provided. This reflects negatively on both the referrer and you.

2. Strategic Relationship Development

There will be opportunities that arise for you to develop an important referrer relationship. Such strategic relationships will often represent the potential for significant referrals to you. Here are three examples of strategic relationships.

A relationship with a workplace near your practice, particularly if the work being done at the workplace is manual in nature, like a factory. If you gain a referral, then follow up with a key person at the workplace and discuss how you can provide further services to them.

Another possible strategic relationship, which I have mentioned previously, is a sports club that needs a local provider to send their injured people to. Such a relationship can be rewarding because, once a relationship is established, they will refer not just players at the club but also staff and those who operate the club. To seal the deal, offer to do a triage session or an information session for the players about whatever aspect of expertise you feel comfortable with. Examples of this might be to talk about footwear if you're a podiatrist or a balanced diet if you're a dietitian. Any healthcare professional can talk about injury prevention or acute injury management, so make sure you offer to do this.

Another possible strategic relationship might be with a local school. Schools employ nurses who look after children who may be injured or sick during school hours. Developing a relationship with the school may result in referrals to you of the injured children.

Always ask this question from a referrer's perspective: What's in it for me? It is not enough to simply say how good you are, if you are not considering what the referrer will achieve from a strategic relationship with you. In a nutshell, a good strategic relationship with your referral involves at least these two things:

- Good letters. Such a letter will concisely convey your assessment, plan for treatment and expected outcomes from your treatment.

- Regular communication. This means not just occasionally contacting referrers but making this activity at least monthly. You cannot build a referral relationship by hitting 'set and forget'. Offering to provide reference articles or new information about your practice are sound methods to keep the relationship fresh.

3. Gifts and Acknowledgement of Good Referrers

Providing acknowledgement or gifts to good referrers is a complicated dynamic and needs to be done with tact and within social conventions. The gift should not be seen as an incentive but a genuine thank you, or a reward and acknowledgement of a referrer's support.

Christmas gifting is common and acceptable. When working with the LifeCare network, we used to send a bottle of wine on behalf of individual clinicians or a hamper to referrers of note from individual practices. In turn, we received gifts from imaging groups and GP practices who we supported.

Individual gifts to a patient who have become an advocate of your practice can also be worthy acknowledgement. The practice could purchase a book of movie tickets, for example, and leave it up to clinicians to assess when they are able to identify someone who is recommending their friends and colleagues to regularly attend the practice. I consider that if a patient has sent three or more of their own contacts to the practice, they should be acknowledged.

4. Made-to-Stick Messaging

I can recommend a book titled *Made to Stick* by Dan and Chip Heath. The book details how best to create messages that will be remembered and stick in people's minds. Such messages can be useful when thinking of doing a promotion at your practice.

The Heath brothers called the best messages 'SUCCES messages'. Where SUCCES is an acronym for:

- **Simple** — the message should not be complicated
- **Unexpected** — something a bit unusual
- **Concrete** — has a beginning and an end
- **Concise** — not too detailed
- **Emotional** — should create an emotional response
- **Stories** — should try to be a narrative story

The authors used an example called 'The Great Kidney Heist' to illustrate this, and I paraphrase:

A person is in a bar having a drink and has their drink spiked. They wake up in a cold bath. There is a notice on the edge of the bath that says: "You are okay. You have had your kidney taken and the tubes coming from your body should be maintained. Your health is not in danger. You should now call 911 on the phone provided and advise the emergency personnel of the location written on the note."

You can decide if this story meets the criteria of a SUCCES message! Be creative and make up a story that fits your practice and why someone should come and see you. The key is to ensure the story should be short enough to be easily recounted to others.

5. RMBD Strategies

When I worked in a practice network (LifeCare) we owned and operated some 15 practices. We developed an education approach that we called: Relationship Marketing Business Development (RMBD).

This involved hourly sessions where we would invite speakers to visit and speak about a variety of topics. Some examples were sales, customer service, creative writing, improving performance, and measuring performance. We would always publish the KPI's of highly regarded performers in these sessions on the topic we were covering to motivate others towards this. These also functioned as examples of what levels could be achieved. We also encouraged questions to be asked of the speaker to aid learning. Overall, we saw RMBD as a growth strategy, an activity that created advocates and was a risk management strategy to prevent negativity around our practice. It was also crucial to see continued growth and improved performance from all our members.

At the time we also learnt some important lessons. For example, we furthered our knowledge around what referrers want from those they refer to. It is well known that GPs like to use radiology/imaging services. Why? Obviously because imaging is crucial to a diagnosis in many instances. There were other important factors that we determined:

- Imaging is usually timely. No waiting to get imaging done (in most cases).
- The GP gets a report from the radiologist in a timely fashion.
- The GP mitigates any risk that they will miss something like a fracture or something more sinister.

Think about the three things above and see how you can apply these principles to your practice.

Ongoing Development of Clinical Excellence

Your development of clinical excellence throughout your practitioner journey is ongoing, there is no end point. You can always improve your knowledge, ability and experience. Some of the important points in developing your clinical excellence have been covered in Stage One, but I think it is worth highlighting the key points that are still relevant to your journey through Stage Two:

Courses or Further Academic Study

There is always another course to do and qualifications to gain. Choose wisely and ask your mentor what you should consider doing next. One day you may be presenting such courses to others as you develop.

Reading

There are many journals that you can access. Some practices provide these for you, but you need to make a plan that will allow you time to read. I recommend that you read at least four articles per month at this stage of your career.

Observation

We have covered this but, as you improve your practice, you need to seek out other clinicians with more experience, so you continue growing your abilities.

Presentations/Conferences

I remember being so scared about presenting. But to improve I just kept taking any opportunity that arose to do so. I even remember practising my presentations in front of my wife before I delivered them. If you want to improve, then push yourself to take the opportunities presented to you. Similarly with conferences. Try to attend one relevant conference per year on top of the lectures and workshops you may attend.

Teaching

Become a teacher to those more junior. When teaching others, you learn how much you know and conversely don't know. Students sharpen your approach and make you think and learn.

Volunteering

Do this particularly when you know others with more experience may also be there, including practitioners from other professions you can learn from. Such events are usually casual and work is team-based, which encourages interaction. By volunteering you develop your network of colleagues just as you do with conferences. I have developed some lifelong friends by attending conferences.

Maximising Your USP with Referrers

You should be developing your USP and you need referrers to know that you have such a USP. The only way to do this is to engage with referrers and tell them your special interest and your USP. When you speak to, communicate or meet your referrer, tell them about your special interest. Advise them that you have read articles about this special interest area and that you have now treated a number of patients with the problem and had good results. Your special interest will then be developing into your USP in your referrer's mind. You will prove to them you have this USP when you treat their patients and get positive results.

Develop Your Personal Branding

We now live in the age of social media. Possibly a good thing but also a potential curse at the same time. We all have an identity and character traits that we use to communicate and perform in our work. How you maximise this identity through social media to help your practice takes time and thought, and how you apply this should be considered and regularly reviewed. Effectively you are creating a brand. You need to control that brand and not have others take it from you or tarnish it. There are so many digital channels you can use to publish and propagate your brand, and I do not intend advising which of these you should ultimately use but I do have some recommendations:

Facebook and Instagram

Create a separate brand profile from your personal profile. Keep the focus on your practice and brand yourself in that context. Knowing what you are good at (your USP) is important to push out into these channels.

LinkedIn

This channel is more for professionals and can be a great forum to show and develop your branding. I know of a practitioner who used this channel to build his practice using these key words: Lower limb, Australian class athletics, the suburb of his practice, tendon injury. He focused on what he was good at, where he worked, and the level of contact he has with a sporting group. He received no fewer than two referrals per week from this branding.

I recommend that you seek advice in the development of your social media presence and your personal website. Also discuss with this professional what channels to use and how best to promote yourself using those channels. I also recommend that you invest in studio quality photos of yourself as these can be used for a variety of different purposes over a ten-year period (providing you keep yourself in good shape!). Ultimately, knowing what you are offering and understanding your audience demographic should assist you to choose the best channels. Facebook may not suit the demographic you wish to attract, unless that demographic is an older cohort, otherwise channels such as Instagram and TikTok may be more suitable. Of course, by the time you read this book there may be many more channels to choose from, so be flexible and — to re-iterate — consult industry experts to stay up to date.

2.2.3 Measurement

> *"You can't improve what you don't measure."*

Is a quote often attributed to Peter Drucker (1909-2005) who is widely accepted as one of the most, if not the most, influential thinkers on business management. This sentence elicits both admiration and plenty of ire because when measurement becomes an end in and of itself, it may consign itself to irrelevance.

I like to call relevant measures Key Performance Indicators (KPI's) and will use this term as we develop this topic. Setting clear objectives is important, but you also need measures that show progress to your objectives. I will detail some measures that I think are highly relevant, but you will need to personalise some of these to suit you and your practice. The key measurement objectives are: Clinical Activities, Commercial Improvement, Administration/Time management, Avoiding Risk, and Career Development.

These objectives are also covered in the Achieving Your Career Objectives document that I have included in Appendix 1, where they are in template form.

Clinical Activities

Your objective might be to learn more about treating spinal conditions. You need to be able to evaluate whether you have learned more about such problems. Your KPI's should direct your performance. Make sure you set KPI's that are binary. You achieve them or you do not. Some examples are: identify and organise to attend a course where the topic is being presented within the next quarter; or read two relevant articles in the next month and review/discuss with someone more experienced than you.

Commercial Improvement

Your objective in this case may be to earn $100K per year. If you break this number down to what gross income you need to earn per week, i.e. $2K per week, we can more easily set some KPI's.

If your fee per patient is $90 and you receive 50% of your fee, we can do the maths to identify the hourly income you need to bill.

For example:

You work 35 hours per week. You see on average 1.8 patients per hour for each of the 35 hours and your average consult fee is $90, then 35 x 1.8 x $90 = $5,670. This is your gross billings figure for a week.

You might receive 50% of these billings. I say 50% because the other 50% is likely to cover the service fee the business owner charges you. In contractor arrangements, the business will provide a room, staff, equipment, patient billing, software and other resources for you. These elements are services and the business charges you a service fee to cover these costs. Such service fees are negotiable with the business. I have used 50% for illustrative purposes in this example.

So we divide your gross billings of $5,670 by 2 = $2,835. This is your net income per week.

Assuming you work 46 weeks per year (four weeks holiday and two weeks public holidays) then $2,835 x 46 weeks = $130,410 income.

Now that you understand the maths, you can see that if you achieve your KPI's for patients per hour, average fee, hours per week, and weeks per year, then you will easily achieve your objective. That said, it is tough to fill 35 hours per week with 1.8 patients each hour, but you can work the maths to suit what you think is possible for you to achieve.

Administration/Time Management

Creating some KPI's for this aspect of your working week is not so easy and will require discipline. I have always advised young clinicians that to achieve a full patient list your KPI should be to spend roughly 10% of the time you have available to do the planning, study, relationship building and analysis that will ensure you achieve a full list. In the case of our example above (working 35 hours per week), this will mean you should spend 3.5 hours per week on these tasks.

It will not work if you think you can squeeze that time in between patients or when someone fails to attend. So once again ... plan time to plan. Sounds a bit strange, but ensure you have the 3.5 hours in your diary as appointments in order to make sure the tasks that are needed are performed.

Once you dedicate this time, you will find it becomes the most productive time you spend. Make sure you follow the time management matrix and use the time well in the not urgent but important quadrant described in Figure 4.

Avoiding Risk

I am not talking about avoiding going out after dark in strange places or surfing giant waves, but ensuring you are mitigating risks in your practice. When you have your 3.5 hours of admin, you can make sure that you have worked on the following: make sure your file notes are complete and are up to date, make sure that you do not have your registration or insurance due or even worse overdue, make sure you are aware of whatever directives may have been advised in your profession regarding infection control or Covid safety, ensure that what type of equipment you might use has been serviced and is in good working order, make sure that you are looking after your own health with a good diet and enough rest, and make clear KPI's for the above and write them down in a planning document.

Career Development

Of course, you do not need to plan your career every month, but your plan should include some objectives. For example, the desire to enrol in a Master's program or a significant course that has been advertised. Your KPI's in this case will be to make sure you do what prerequisites are required to enrol. Make sure you understand the costs involved and have a plan to finance that. You may ask the practice where you work to assist you to finance this course. No harm in asking.

You may not achieve all of your objectives; they need to be realistic and getting sound advice from your trusted mentor when setting them will ensure that most of your objectives will be met. Determining how long to persist in achieving a particular objective can be challenging and your mentor can help you with this. There's little point banging your head against a brick wall if you know you can't break through. At this point, objectives should be re-evaluated. For example, you may have enrolled in a postgraduate program and your personal circumstances might have changed, e.g. you have a child or suffer an illness and this prevents you from either affording or finding the time to finish the program.

2.2.4 Marketing Plan

Developing a clear, objective and achievable marketing plan will keep you focused and on track to achieve commercial success. It will allow you to do such things as see weekly growth of your patient list and fill your appointment times across your week, rather than just filling up early mornings or late evenings when the demand for treatment is often greater. It will also provide direction and milestones for you to follow and achieve. It is also something that you can share with mentors and colleagues to gain their feedback, because input from others while you are working towards commercial success is very important. I have included an actual plan developed by two young clinicians in the outer west of Melbourne to provide some ideas for you:

A good marketing plan should cover the following details:

Targets
Identify the potential referrers you wish to target. Identify who already refers to you. Such targets might be: doctors, other allied health clinicians, schools, businesses, sporting teams, specialists, and so on.

Actions
What action you or others will take to identify how you plan to engage with the targets. This will include identifying the best channels to reach targets, such as digital, letters, visits, brochures.

By Whom
Nominate who will actually do the work!

By When
A timeframe is crucial to keep you on track. If your approach is a 'call-to-action' campaign, then the timeline will determine for how long you are making a specific offer available. A call-to-action campaign is a plan that has a special offer, will expire in a short timeframe and is compelling.

Outcomes

Counting and measuring what you do is one of the good habits we have talked about. Make sure you have binary outcomes that will be able to be measured.

Marketing Plan Examples

The details below can be used by you for your practice or when you look to start a clinic of your own. The following two examples are detailed to indicate some options that can be employed.

Example 1

Target market:

- Enhanced Primary Care EPC (Government-funded referrals from General Practitioners)
- Private referrals

Current client sources:

- Mr and Mrs X — Plaza Medical Centre
- Dr Y — Plaza Medical Centre

Potential client sources:

- Client direct referral — patients attending Plaza Medical Centre (A)
- Current client referral via word-of-mouth (B)

- Business owners/employees of retail stores of Centro (C)
- Shoppers of Centro (D)
- Local residential area (Keilor Downs, St Albans, Kealba) (E)
- Aged care population — hostels, nursing homes, local (F)

Short-term goals:
1) 5 x new EPC referrals per week via EPC marketing campaign (8-10 weeks)
2) 1 x new private patient per week via private patient marketing campaign (8-10 weeks)
3) Patients per hour KPI — 2 (8-10 weeks)
4) Revenue per hour — $150 (8-10 weeks)
5) Total revenue per month — $4,000 (8-10 weeks) (Currently approx $2,500/month)

Note: $75 revenue per patient

Long-term goals:
- Recruit 1 equivalent full-time physiotherapist — goal 10 patients per day within a year

Strategies:

Enhanced Primary Care marketing campaign
- Maintain relationships with local doctor referrers
- Offer free initial musculoskeletal screening program — refer to GP — when patient commences EPC program

- Produce attractive, professional, colour brochure specifically targeted at potential EPC patients — graphic design and printing costs (to be discussed)
- Distribution:
  - Liaise with Plaza receptionist staff to give GP patients an accompanying brochure
  - Liaise with Centro Centre management regarding:
    - opportunities of networking with Centro employers/employees
    - handing out of brochures in the shopping centre
    - sandwich board consent
    - Deliver to mailboxes in local area (How to recruit mail walkers?)

Private Patient Marketing Campaign
- Produce cost-effective black and white A5 brochures
- Sandwich board
- Walk-ins
- Social media campaign, ad words, carousel ads, develop monthly budget with consultant

Weekly marketing activities:
- Tabulate new patient data — i.e. rows (source); columns (week no.)
- Evaluate results monthly and review activities above

Example 2

The second example below is from a Lifecare practice and covers what the practice needs to do internally to prepare their campaign.

Internal practice resource development.
1. Ensure handouts are up to date in marketing package including:
- Practitioner's Speciality Card
- Handouts on all classes run
- EPC information/care plan
- Referral pad (currently being reprinted)
- Information on Spinal Pain Management services, digital and paper notices.
2. Print new Practice Newsletter (current stocks are running low). Include articles introducing new practitioners/class schedule/bulk billing of EPC, renovation and improvements at practice, etc.
3. Update inhouse signage listing practitioners.
4. Continue to send new patients welcome letter.
- Display practice newsletter, renovation updates, class schedule and handouts on hydro and Pilates in all waiting rooms.

Teaching Resources Needed

1. Michael to meet regularly with practitioners bringing them up to date on practice events/new practitioners, ensuring open lines of communication between practitioners.
2. John to introduce new practitioners to staff and current practitioners emphasising their particular areas of interest in memo/profile format.
3. Nicole to encourage Dr Stuart to meet physios on a regular basis to exchange knowledge and treatment ideas.

2.3 Why is Commercial Success Important?

In much of the material above I have discussed certain aspects of the importance of commercial success. I will now go into more detail about why it is important under the following headings: Income, Learning, and Opportunity.

Income

As you work on your commercial practice success, you will see that your take-home income will increase. It is important that this occurs, as this progress will keep you engaged, animated and enthusiastic to continue learning and developing new skills. From my experience, it is a key part of career building. Being caring, helpful and giving back to your profession and community is important, but so is increasing your income to provide choices for you in your lifestyle.

Learning

During university/college study it is unlikely that you received much commercial training. Given some 80 % of all allied health practitioners move into private practice, the ability to learn commercial and business skills is crucial and will help keep you engaged in your chosen profession. The outcome from this work will be increased job satisfaction and engagement.

Opportunity

There is a myriad of possible opportunities that come from achieving clinical excellence and commercial success. If you are seen as a patient list builder and list owner, then your options for different work opportunities increase. List builders and owners manage to be busy wherever they practise, and understanding the basic skills of list development can be applied wherever they work.

Some of the other opportunities are:

Elite Sport Attachment

Those who have acquired the skills I've outlined up to now are seen as well organised, good communicators, motivated and eager to learn. Sporting teams at both elite and grassroots levels are always looking for people with these skills.

Lecturing and Course Delivery

You will be seen as someone who has more to offer beyond patient treatment, and you may be asked to lecture about a particular topic or support a specialist who conducts their own courses for others.

Credibility

Others will look up to you when they are aware that you have knowledge and have a busy list of patients. This will see you called upon to mentor others and share what you have learnt.

Progression

It is harder to progress to Stage Three if you are not both clinically excellent and commercially successful in your own practice. If you harbour the ambition to operate a practice with others, achieving clinical excellence and commercial success is the pathway you need to follow.

2.4 What Else Do I Need to Achieve Commercial Success?

The are other activities in addition to those I've already outlined that will assist you to achieve commercial success. They are:

Hard Work

I have presented many examples of the work you need to do if you are to be successful. Underpinning this is the capacity to apply yourself and work hard. After three to five years (plus) of completing Stage One as a practitioner, it may seem a big thing to ask to continually re-apply yourself diligently to learning new skills. I understand this, but I ask that you start a major and complex process with a clear vision of the final goal you aim to achieve. Even now, thinking about your ultimate exit should never be out of focus. What you do will set your career trajectory and provide choices for you along the journey. The key will be planning, the seeking of mentors, employing good time management practices, and enthusiasm.

Active Listening

There are five levels of listening:

Ignoring: The lowest level of listening is called ignoring — not listening at all.

Pretend Listening: Pretend listening is most easily explained in the face-to-face conversation. You're talking to the other person and they have that 'backpacking in Brazil' look in their eyes, i.e. their thoughts are elsewhere. This form of listening is often employed by parents when their two-year-old is talking incessantly upon learning to talk.

Selective Listening: During selective listening we pay attention to the speaker as long as they are talking about things we like or agree with.

Attentive Listening: Attentive listening occurs when we carefully listen to the other person, but, while they are speaking, we are deciding whether we agree or disagree, often determining when they are about to stop talking.

Empathetic Listening: This is the fifth and highest level of listening. I sometimes call empathetic listening 'active listening'. At this level you are not just listening with the intention to reply, but actually putting yourself in the shoes of those whom you are listening to.

Make sure you work on your listening skills and remember that old adage that God gave us two ears and one mouth so we would listen twice as much as we talk. It takes awareness to know that what you are listening to is important, so be aware of those who mentor you, your colleagues, and those dear to you, to ensure you get the most from these relationships by actively listening. You will be surprised how much you will learn.

Application of Your Knowledge

It is good to develop skills and knowledge that you can apply to your practice. The key word is application. This means trying some new things like applying a new treatment, or considering other options like discussing or even referring your patient to another experienced colleague or mentor for their opinion. Such action will not be viewed negatively by your patient. They will see that you are open to other suggestions about how best to treat their problem or condition.

Personal Development

Development of self and your capabilities beyond those required for your professional life will expand your horizons and stimulate your growth. Read widely and listen actively to those whose opinions you value. Explore different aspects of health practice and do not be afraid to experiment with your thoughts so that your work is enriched with new ideas. There are many self-development and self-awareness courses that you can attend that will assist your planning and establish new ways you can grow.

Reading Your Patients' Needs

Some years ago I visited one of the network practices to view the progress that practice was making. The practice was in the city and the clinician and practice partner was a manipulative therapist named Chris. He saw many patients from the legal profession and corporate businesses located in the CBD. Such patients would be time poor and would often ring to be seen between legal cases or meetings and wanted to be attended to quickly and effectively. Chris had the manual therapy and assessment skills that allowed him to diagnose the problem quickly and provide appropriate manual therapy or manipulation to the affected joint or structure that was at fault. Chris read that to thrive in such an environment he would need to manage his time well and have his patients in and out of his clinic in 20 minutes or so. The patients raved about Chris and he received many word-of-mouth referrals by reading the needs of his clientele.

Responding to Your Patients' Requests

My daughter has a chronic problem with migraines. She is also a medical student and has had significant rehabilitation for several musculoskeletal injuries. Her migraines were helped with deep-tissue massage from masseuses and myotherapists. When she moved interstate, she attended a new service and advised the practitioner that: "I have had massage therapy before, and when the practitioner does certain treatments they are very effective in treating my migraines." She visited three different practitioners before she found one whom responded to what she requested and delivered that treatment. She was very clear in what treatment she wanted and expected, but those first practitioners either did not listen or chose not to listen. My message here is that, after your assessment, it is fine to want to provide certain treatments that you deem will be helpful, but make sure you respond to the patient's request first. That's the starting point to ensure your patient returns for their next treatment.

We have now completed Stage Two of the practitioner journey. Some of you may choose to stop in your journey here and simply continue to develop your own practice or be successful as practitioners working in the businesses of others. This will provide you with great satisfaction and, provided you are clinically excellent and develop the skills we have identified in this stage, you will become commercially successful and thrive as you will be in the position of owning your list.

If you want the journey to continue to the next stage then read on. I will now take you into Stage Three where we will explore how you can lead your list to maximise your equity and learn another set of skills.

3.0 STAGE THREE

Leading Your List — Maximise Equity

The Health Practitioner's Journey™

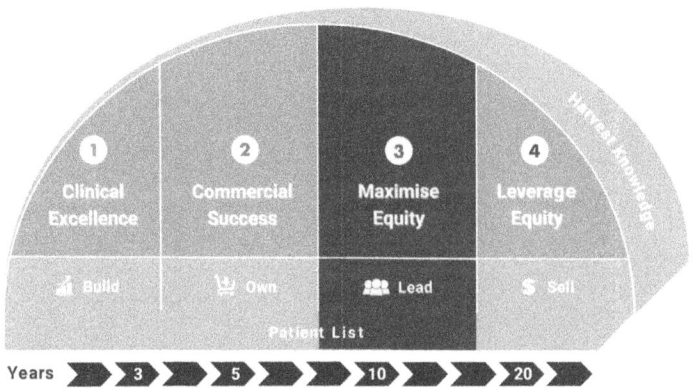

Stage Three will cover the important steps to starting and developing your own business. To be at Stage Three you will have developed a practice that is busy and is now owned by you. This next stage is about using the clinical excellence and commercial success you have developed to create a business. By this I mean operating a clinic that you will not only work in, but also employ others and operate and develop on a commercial basis.

It is crucial to identify those who are passionate to move

to Stage Three. This step isn't for everyone and you may be content to achieve clinical excellence and commercial success and stay working without embarking on this stage.

3.1 Who is Stage Three For?

Achieving the first two stages is mandatory before moving to Stage Three. To reinforce my point above: this stage is for those who have achieved clinical excellence and commercial success in practice.

I see the elements of clinical excellence and commercial success as being two halves of a whole for a successful practitioner:

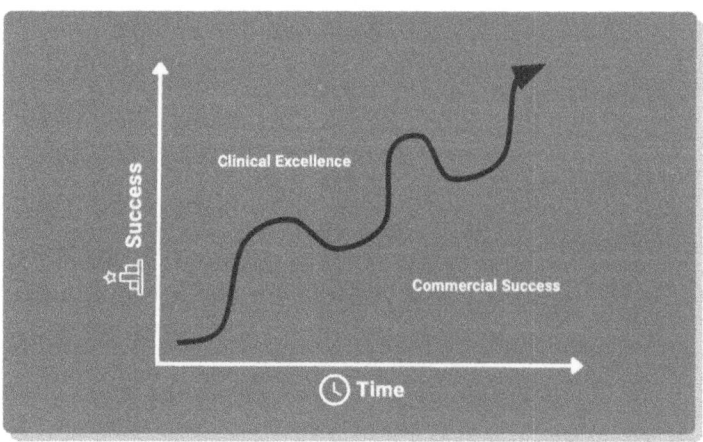

Figure 11: Two Halves of a Whole

Having these elements prepares you to focus on Stage Three. There are some other traits that identify who this stage is for:

Motivation

I've spoken about motivation and hard work earlier in this book. It is important that at this stage in your practitioner journey you are motivated to do the work because there's a lot to do in this stage.

Desire to Develop an Asset

This might sound a little boring or corporate, but having something that you own is stimulating and exciting. An asset, once established, will enable you to make money by more than just the fruit of seeing patients. Others will work with you to develop your business and hence grow your asset.

Fits into Your Plans for Your Future

If you see your future as travelling the world, working only when you need money, you should be looking to start building the asset. That said, the asset may in time enable you to have greater financial freedom to do the things you want. I have consulted with a couple who took their practices and developed a large business in the west of New South Wales. They worked hard over a number of years to start and build this business. When they decided to take a six-month sabbatical to France with their children, they entrusted the management of the business to some of their staff. The business was still thriving when they returned as they had worked hard to establish a good business that could operate without their day-to-day input.

You Have the Resources, Energy, Time and Passion

The resources you need to establish a business include funding or access to funding, some good advisors to assist you, and research to explore locations. Doing such activities takes energy and time, often while you are still working in the hands-on capacity of seeing patients. Being passionate about this step is important, as I have mentioned, but it should be something you dream about. Just this week I received an email from a podiatrist whom we shall call Jill. She asked me when she should look to fulfil her dream to start her own practice. I discussed clinical excellence and commercial success, the need for a mentor, and the timing she was thinking of. She works as a practitioner in a good business where she is learning, and she said she was thinking that after five years from graduation she would embark on owning her own business. I considered Jill's response to timing and relayed to her that, provided she continued to develop her practice and was learning, there was no hurry and that her timeline was appropriate. The timing to take action and commence the work needed to establish a business is a personal one, and only you can decide when you have sufficient resources, energy, time and passion.

You Feel Ready

I was approached by a couple who had worked in a network of practices I was operating. They were highly regarded and had developed their skills as practitioners and had developed Unique Selling Propositions. They had shown a capacity to teach others in that network and expressed a desire to move forward to the next logical step. That logical step for them was to seek a new opportunity where they could develop a business together.

They made a sea change and started to work with another practice network. This step established them in the location they had chosen. I assisted them to negotiate with the owner of that network to buy the practice they were working in. They have since thrived, starting another business and they are currently in the process of building a purpose-built facility that formed part of their dream. I have continued to be their business mentor for six years and continue to advise them as needed. In this case, a lifestyle near the beach was a motivator for them, and developing their business supports the lifestyle they have chosen.

It is not always possible to know when you are ready, so don't despair if you are thinking, "I will never be ready." Life challenges us all the time, but sometimes you need to back yourself and take a chance. I hope to assist you to take that chance with a solid foundation and will provide the tools you need to do so.

3.2 What is Maximising Equity?

You have a taste of what commercial success can mean by owning your list. This means that you can confidently develop a list of patients that is sustainable wherever you may go. You have your own equity embedded in your ability to own your list and now you can look to maximise that equity by setting up your own business, rather than working in someone else's practice or network of practices. By establishing your own business, you will have control over developing that business as you see fit. It will be a part of you and your vision, and over time you will make profits (that is the goal, at the least), you will own something to be proud of, and something that you can sell when it's time. Maximising your equity means developing an investment grade asset that will be attractive for someone to buy or will attract a network to make it part of their growth plans.

There are five elements that are equally important in leading your list and maximising your equity. It is wise to make sure you are not missing one of these as you move forward. They are: Owning the Business, Establishing a Greenfield Business, Growing the Business, Managing the Business and Long-Term Planning.

3.2.1 Owning the Business

There are three options when the time is right for you to own your business.

- Buying into the business that you are working within (either buying a part equity share or buying the practice outright from the owner).
- Buying an existing business that you are not currently working in.
- Setting up your greenfield practice business.

I will address the detail of buying into the current business you are working within or buying into an existing business together because both investments are very similar.

Buying into Existing Businesses

There are multiple factors to address in this instance that I have grouped under the following headings: The Price, Finance, Due Diligence, and Contract of Sale.

The Price

The price you negotiate to pay for such an investment (known as your equity) will be based on a combination of several factors:

1. Profitability of the Business

The usual measure of profit or sustainable earnings is detailed in the acronym EBITDA. This acronym stands for:

- Earnings Before Interest, Tax, Depreciation and Amortisation
- Earnings is the difference between the gross billings of the business, less expenses such as professional labour, admin staff, rent, leasing, etc.
- Interest is the interest earned by the practice on the earnings.
- Tax is the required government tax that is levied on profits.
- Depreciation is a charge that is made on capital goods bought like furniture, equipment, computers, and so on. There are rules about the depreciation charge based on the life of an asset. For example, a treatment plinth is considered to have a long life since it does not wear out and hence the cost will be depreciated over 15 years with one fifteenth of the cost being depreciated each year.
- Amortisation is similar to depreciation but relates to goodwill that has been paid to buy a business.

The above detail may seem complex if you have not operated a business. There are accounting rules and formalities that accountants are required to work within. At this time you need to know that a valuation of a business should be based on a multiple of the EBITDA value. Having an accountant assist you in the process of buying a business will be important for you to understand the risks involved when you purchase a business, and to be sure that you pay a fair price. For example, these days healthcare practice businesses sell for a multiple of the EBITDA. The multiple will vary, based on a number of factors, e.g. the profitability of the business, the database of clients, the location and length of operation of the business, the practice gross billings, the quality of the fit-out, and so on. In allied health practices the range of the multiple is between 2.5 and 5 x EBITDA.

2. Size of the Practice and Quality of the Facility

The square meterage of the business will allow for growth and expansion of services and hence the growth will not be limited by space. More space is not always of value as it can mean that there is much unused space, which will not increase the business billings. The quality of the facility is important because patients will acknowledge facility quality as an expectation of the price they will pay for the services provided.

3. The Database of Patients Attending the Business

A sizable and well-maintained patient database that can be readily accessed is a business asset. This database can provide access to the patients' details, which can be used easily for promotions, email blasts and social media.

4. Location

A location near other healthcare services will mean that people can assess that location easily. Parking and ease of access is important for a business and will attract patients. Good visibility from the streetscape and passing foot and vehicle traffic will also mean that patients will notice the business and hence be more likely to use the services provided.

5. Business Billings

The gross billings figure of a practice is an indication not only of the business's viability, but also suggest whether the business has reliable systems, existing staff and hence greater potential to grow and be profitable. This is not always the case but, as a general rule, a business that is grossing billings north of $1,000,000 may be a better investment than a business grossing $200,000 because the larger business will be able to cover costs of operating the business and generate greater sustainable earnings. Of course, this will also mean that the valuation of such a business will be higher.

6. Brand

Brand value is very much a perception, but awareness of a business will often lead to a higher value of that business. Higher awareness will mean more clients and greater opportunity for growth. This assumes that the brand is indeed healthy and not tarnished, i.e. the business is well known for all the wrong reasons. It is hard to place a monetary value on brands, but you should still consider the brand when looking at the possible value of the business.

7. Leverage

You will have a list of patients and a good reputation (based on the work you have done in Stages One and Two), which will assist in your purchase negotiations. If you are known to have these attributes, then you will be seen as an asset to the business and this may mean that the price you pay to purchase may be discounted. Using such leverage may be viewed as a bold move, but it is something to be considered.

8. Restraint

Most work contracts and particularly contracts of sale will include some restraint clauses. These restraints will detail the expectations of the business and your responsibilities as a new business equity partner. Such matters as the expected hours you need to work and the need to be open and transparent about any perceived or real conflicts of interest, for example, owning equity in another similar business may need to be disclosed. If you are not a majority partner in the business, then there will be a restraint about setting up another practice within a defined distance (usually three to five kilometres). Another restraint will be to not encourage staff or practitioners at the practice to leave or go elsewhere should you decide to sell your equity and leave the business. Be aware that the issues above are real and will need to be negotiated in your contract to purchase business equity.

I am aware of many situations where practitioners wished to leave a business they were working in or sell their equity, but restraint clauses meant they could not practice where they wanted to for a year or more.

9. The Expectations of the Exiting Practice Owner

It is important to know what the current business owner plans to do when you become an equity partner. In a larger business there may be a number of partners and it may not matter too much if one chooses to leave, retire, or change their role. In smaller practices this matter is more important, as you need to know the roles that you and the exiting partner(s) will play. The sharing of the many duties should be fair and equitable. For example, who will perform staff management, education, recruitment induction, marketing, and so on? Open and honest conversations before you commit to purchase equity are important and be sure you have all the detail and information before you make any commitment.

Given all of the above, a valuation is still a negotiation. As a guideline, healthcare businesses will sell based on a multiple of sustainable earnings. The size of the multiple will be determined by the factors detailed above. Having an advisor should assist you to make the right decisions and pay a fair price.

Finance

Once you have negotiated the price, you then need to finance your business purchase. Buying a business is a big decision. There is a reason that most people never embark on owning, opening, developing and growing a business. It can be stressful, take significant time and money, and will need your constant attention. In my opinion it is worth it for the satisfaction and potential wealth creation it can provide. Access to finance is necessary and having a number of options to finance is ideal, although not always possible.

If you have saved up some money, it is a consideration to use some of that nest egg to make the purchase. Borrowing from family and friends is also an option. This option needs careful consideration as you do not want to be in a position where doing this will affect your relationships or place pressure on those who are close to you. Borrowing from a bank or finance institution is a clear path and there are many finance lenders you can approach. Often your professional association can also assist with recommendations. Making sure you can meet the repayments is crucial, as is understanding that you may need help to guarantee any loan you apply for. Family can be very helpful with guarantees even if they are unable to provide a loan for you.

Due Diligence

The process of working out an acceptable value for a business purchase is known as performing due diligence. This is a formal process that determines that the value you have priced actually exists. It will determine things like how well set-up the existing business is, how well organised it is and, importantly, determine the future earnings you are able to make from the business. I recommend this activity for any business purchase large or small. There are a number of factors to consider and the list below, although very detailed, is a guide to the things that you should investigate or ask for as part of the purchasing process. The detail below was an actual due diligence process used before contract of sale and purchase price was agreed. I won't go into every detail listed below because I've provided this simply to give you some direction about things that should be considered when looking to purchase outright or into an existing business.

Detailed P&L reports:
- Last three financial years
- Details of any adjustments made/required, i.e. total $ payments to owners, and in what form were payments made
- Other personal expenses included in reports
- Monthly breakdown of previous year

Current year budget
- Same format as P&L's mentioned above
- Monthly breakdown if possible

Latest current year financials:
- In particular, current revenue details:

Income breakdown:
- By income stream/product, if multiple services
- By clinician/contractor
- In particular, billings of owners, impact on current business
- By month

Current fee schedule

Any KPI reporting/history

Access to current/historical KPI information, i.e.
- Chargeable hours per clinician/contractor per month
- Revenue per clinician/contractor per month
- Top 10 customers/referrers, billings per month
- Actuals/Targets/Budgets per month

Referral patterns, i.e.
- Referrals per month, broken down for review

Top 10 customers:

- Breakdown by services provided
- Breakdown by consultant
- Monthly breakdown if possible

Details of marketing/ promotion activities undertaken in region:

- $ spent
- In which areas
- Results/outcomes achieved

Current staff clinician/contractor listing:

- Profession
- Length of service at Practice
- Experience
- Current employment contract details/remuneration
- Staff turnover rates
- Contract would be conditional on all/most staff coming across
- To work for new entity on similar conditions
- Like to meet staff at appropriate stage, assess, etc

Job description/details of admin staff roles:

- Similar details of all admin staff
- Areas covered, responsibilities, duties
- Capabilities
- Possible double up with HNA centre

Future plans of owners:

- Do they want to stay involved in the business?
- In what capacity, i.e. clinical hours, admin/ management?
- For how long?
- Initial thoughts on transition, handover issues

Accreditation details

Details of all Insurance/Agent Preferred Provider Panels
Overview of current IT systems:

- Accounting/ payroll systems used
- IT Infrastructure in place
- Software licences, IT security in place
- Phone, fax, email systems in place

Summary of current insurances

Current property details:

- Owned, available for long-term lease
- Current market rates
- Motor vehicle costs included in P&L's above

Leased, details of current lease terms

- included in P&L's above

Review of detailed balance sheet at the time:

- Preference would be to acquire the operating business
- Current plant and equipment, fixed asset listing

- Details of any finance arrangements on this equipment
- This is generally paid out by owners on settlement
- Details of current business name registration, for transfer
- Details of current website address, for transfer

Owner's thoughts on percentage of business to be sold:

- Buyer's preference is to acquire 60-80% of business
- Owners to retain balance
- Both parties to continue to work together for mutual benefit

Contract of Sale

There will be a contract of sale developed between you and the owner that should detail every aspect of the sale. Having a lawyer assist you is essential. The contract will detail what needs to be paid and when. It may detail that the investment can be paid off by a number of different methods. For example, you may be able to pay by instalments upon making a deposit. At LifeCare we made arrangements in some instances for the purchaser to make equity payments from the dividends they shared from the quarterly practice profits. They did not receive the dividend, but their share of profits was used to pay off the practice equity payment over time.

There is likely to be two further documents that will be needed if a sale is to occur.

A partnership agreement will detail how you and your partner(s) will work together in the business. This agreement should confirm the roles the partners have in the business and the expectation of how those roles will be performed. As a practitioner you will have a service contract that governs how you will be remunerated for your work as a practitioner and what other activities you can perform with mentoring and teaching of staff and practitioners.

Once all of the above has been agreed, then another document will need to set the date to execute the contract of sale and other agreements. This will obviously include a payment for the equity that you will receive. Simply put, you will pay some money and the business will deliver you shares if the business entity is a company, units if a unit trust, or a share of the partnership if that is the structure. Discussing the structure of the business is something that is best done with your lawyers because different structures have different implications for tax, dividends and how you enter and exit the business if that happens at a later date.

3.2.2 Establishing a Greenfield Business

A greenfield business is one that will be started from scratch. Establishing your own business is a two-stage process. First, you create the idea of your ideal practice in your head and then you commit the plan you have to paper.

The advantage of establishing a greenfield practice business is that you will have autonomy in the business, which you can control and grow the way you desire to establish an asset that you may be able to sell one day.

The disadvantages are that, with autonomy, you may lack a close colleague to work with and operating a practice can be a significant burden due to the amount of work required to build up the business from scratch. Starting a practice also comes with the following obligations:

- Council permits may be needed to operate a business in a particular location.
- You will need a range of insurances like professional indemnity for the business and public liability for anything that may go wrong at the practice.
- Development of contracts for staff.
- The need for property and equipment leases.

I will now talk about establishing your greenfield business under two headings: Planning Your Greenfield Business, and Starting Your Greenfield Business.

Planning Your Greenfield Business

Business planning is an essential part of any business. Many think that if you are a health professional all you have to do is to hang out your shingle, open the door and the people will come. This is not the case if you wish to have a sustainable business. Alice in Wonderland beautifully sums up why we need to know where we want to go (and I paraphrase):

Alice: "Would you tell me, please, which way I ought to go from here?"
The Cat: "That depends a good deal on where you want to get to."
Alice: "I don't much care where."
The Cat: "Then is does not matter which way you go."

Another way of looking at planning is to think about building or making renovations to a house. In this instance you will have a plan. You will want to know what it will cost. You will want to know how long it will take and how your cashflow payments need to be made to the builder, and so on. First, you will picture how you want things to look, then sketches will be made and then the plan formulated. All of this occurs before you get the plan approved and quotes from the builder.

The following comments may assist you to further see the benefit of having a good plan. A sound business plan:

- Will improve your chances of being successful (as mentioned earlier in this book, there is evidence

that those who have written goals are more likely to achieve them).
- Will give you the timeline and workflow involved in the set-up and/or improvement of your practice. This will keep you focused on the outcome.
- Should incorporate others who will contribute and support you.
- Increases the efficiency of your time management.
- Gives you a reference point to refer back to, as time goes by.
- Is an ongoing business development tool.
- Is a map to help the business move from where it is now to where you want it to be in the future.

Planning considerations for your greenfield business involve a number of aspects:

Your Current Situation

Your Vision, Mission, Objectives and Strategy
- Core Competencies

External Environment Analysis
- Location
- Resources

I will now elaborate on these aspects.

Your Current Situation

A good way to start your planning is to review where you are now. To do this you can consider doing a SWOT analysis. SWOT stands for Strengths, Weaknesses, Opportunities, Threats. Such analysis will help you critically assess the current state of your practice. Identifying your strengths and weaknesses is very important. Once weaknesses and threats have been identified, you can then go about finding solutions. By way of example, setting up where there are many competitors to your business can be both an opportunity and a threat. The skill here is working out whether it is an opportunity because a concentration of like businesses in a location can have significant drawing power.

You may also wish to conduct an analysis based on Porter's Five Forces, a well-known model named after Harvard Business School professor Michael E Porter, which is a more contemporary approach to assessing your current situation. Specifically, the five forces are:

1) Competition in the Industry

2) Potential of New Entrants

3) Power of Suppliers

4) Power of Customers

5) Threat of Substitute Products

All of these forces have relevance to healthcare businesses and it is absolutely essential for you to assess each of these when considering the establishment of a greenfield practice.

Your Vision, Mission, Objectives and Strategy

Try not to get caught up by definitions or jargon too much. Many books are available to help you understand these terms and develop relevant detail around the concepts they embody. The adage KISS (Keep It Simple, Stupid) applies here! Everyone has seen meaningless vision and mission statements on the foyer walls of businesses. The key is to create something that has meaning for those who will work with you and those who will visit your practice. The following thoughts should give you some guidance about these words and how you can apply them to your practice:

Vision

Ideally your vision is where you want to get to or how you see your business at the end of the planning period and in the future. For example: "To create a practice that sustainably serves the needs of my community." These are powerful words that will direct you to understand: who your community is, what your fee structure will be, and the demand for your business in the community that you will be located in.

Mission

Your mission establishes the type of business you want to create. It should provide some details of the services you wish to provide. For example: "Over the next 24 months my practice will develop a community of supportive referrers, provide a breadth of services in allied health disciplines that will provide acute injury treatment, group classes and rehabilitation in a client friendly environment." This statement implies a timeframe to achieve your vision and the essential requirements you need to make the practice viable.

Values

What is truly important to you? Do you value kindness, consideration, fairness, good communication, ethical behaviour, and so on? It is worth workshopping with others what values you want to exhibit in your business operation.

Objectives

Clearly stated objectives are crucial to your practice and for the people working with you. As discussed in Stage One, adhere to the idea of SMART objectives being: Specific, Measurable, Achievable, Realistic, and Timely.

Core Competencies

The area of core competency is concerned with understanding what you consider you and your business will be good at doing, so you can maximise the commercial advantage that this presents.

Core competencies can lead to commercial advantage if identified and then used in the development of your business. Such competencies are business/practice strengths that meet three tests: Sustainability, Relevance and Uniqueness:

- Sustainability: meaning they are able to be accessed by a wide variety of market segments, e.g. sports clubs, schools, referrers, and so on, for the long term. Relationships with referrer groups take time to develop. An example would be your business is able to offer provision for an appointment to a new referrer and a reply letter to such referrers the same day. By responding on the same day, the referrer will remember you and your business and be more likely to refer again. The referrer will be able to have up-to-date information about what their patient can expect from your business, which is very important in the provision of optimal care.
- Relevance: meaning they are able to make a contribution to the perceived benefit of what you offer. An example of this would be a capacity to cater for patients with poor mobility by having easy access like good parking and a lift, if not on a ground floor, and so on.

- Uniqueness: meaning they are difficult to duplicate by a competitor, so that they cannot take that market segment from your practice. For example, you may have the only piece of equipment of its type available in your region.

It would be very useful for you to also consider having some practitioners in your practice with core competencies in unique skills. For example, a physio with vestibular special interest or speciality, a podiatrist with special training in paediatrics, or a manual therapist who can provide deep-tissue therapy. If they have a unique selling proposition, it may be hard for another practice to offer such a service as there are such few practitioners with this skill.

External Environment Analysis

The external environment refers to issues such as the state of the economy, government policies and the role of regulatory bodies. It is important that an analysis of the external environment considers factors that can have a major impact on business performance. This analysis should include:

- Competitors. Make a phone call to practices/businesses near your proposed site and get an idea of how you are greeted, what information you are provided with, the fees that are being charged, and the unique services being offered.

- The current political climate. What policies exist that may be an opportunity or a threat. Measures such as the Consumer Price Index for the healthcare industry is usually twice that of the general economy. Certain government policies, namely in industrial relations, may impact your practice. Being aware of the issues surrounding engaging staff and practitioners as employees vs contractors is also important.
- Rules and regulations locally and further afield. You may need permits for signage, hours of opening, and so on.
- The economy in general and, more particularly, how your geographic area is faring. Detailed demographic studies of particular suburbs are available at a reasonable cost from government agencies such as the Bureau of Statistics.
- Technological developments. The pace of change is rapid and consideration should be given to technological change, e.g. a paperless environment, the provision of appointment opportunities online, telehealth, and so on.

Location

Where do you wish to start your business? Do you have a specific suburb in mind or a broad area 'north of the city'? The type of practice you want is also relevant to its location and this is something to deal with when you create your vision for your business. For example, if you wish to provide rehabilitation with group classes, women's health, injury rehab, biomechanical analysis with a lab, then the premises will need to be large enough to accommodate this, and good planning will be needed with your fit-out to ensure you have work spaces that are carefully organised.

The cost per square metre of your location is also important. This cost will vary depending on the area or suburb you are located in and the size of the premises. Sometimes if a premise is part of a new development, you can negotiate a rent-free period which can assist greatly. Obtaining a permit to operate a business is mandatory and the permit will specify how many car spaces you need, the hours of operation, and so on.

Resources

What will you need to have in terms of people, financial and physical resources?

Your people

How difficult will it be to recruit the additional people you want? Do you know how to recruit them? Often using social media channels where professional people look, such as LinkedIn or specific online recruitment sites like Seek will be useful, as will asking colleagues and exploring the networks you have established. Be mindful of using recruitment consultants as the service can be expensive. If you do use a consulting firm make sure you do some of your own screening of the applicants. Your interview process should be thorough so that you optimally match the person for the job. I will go into more detail later about recruitment in the Managing the Business section.

Financial resources

How much capital do you have? Do you need to borrow? Who will lend to you? As a general rule, having 10% more capital than you think you need is a good guideline for a sustainable business start-up. Remember that you will need to anticipate CAPEX (Capital Expenditure, i.e. the likely expenses for the major resources you need to purchase in the long term), as well as OPEX (Operating Capital, the day-to-day expenses required to run the business and meet everyday costs, like staff wages, printing supplies, and so on.

In other words, start-up capital is required to set up the business, then working capital will be needed for day-to-day expenditure. Many businesses make this mistake, i.e. allowing for funding to cover the equipment and structural set-up, but leaving no funds to run the business day-to-day.

All financial institutions will provide funding for professional people as they see the health industry as low risk. Make sure you do your due diligence with the help of an accountant. The areas of leasing, bank overdrafts, business loans, and so on, are complex and I recommend you be guided by the professionals. A good rule of thumb is that you need working capital to cover your needs for the first three months without creating any billings.

Physical resources

What equipment will you need to acquire? How do you rate your proposed premises? What front-desk software will you use? What suppliers will you need? What is an effective branding strategy for both the business and your practitioners? Most patients seeking healthcare services will make online searches, so is your website optimised for using search engines? The above questions need to be addressed and the answers depend on your professional discipline, the type of business you wish to build, the expected scope of services, and so on.

Starting Your Greenfield Business

The next step will focus on getting started, executing the plan and implementing the strategy. I have created an indicative non-specific checklist below that may assist you in making sure that all the elements involved with commencing a practice are covered. Study this list before reading the specific comments made below. A few years ago I used a list like this when I was invited to assist a hospital group in Bali, Indonesia, with establishing a multidisciplinary sports medicine centre in one of their hospitals. This list was addressed at weekly meetings and became a critical working document. I ensured one of the doctors involved in the project 'owned' that checklist and this made my job easier by ensuring that all activities were systematically ticked off in a timely manner. The centre opened on time without a hitch.

Put another way, I mentioned the work of Stephen Covey earlier and one of his recommended habits is to "put first things first". In this context, what is meant is to take out your plan and look at what you need to achieve in the first week, the second week, and so on. Once this is done, you will gain a feel for when the practice will realistically be able to open. The opening date will create the timeline of activity. Many fail to achieve their timelines because they fail to execute their stated weekly tasks.

Figure 12: Example of a working checklist

KEY SET-UP AREAS
BRANDING
Signage — exterior and interior
Paintwork in themed branding colours
Sandwich board for promotions

KEY SET-UP AREAS
Practice brochure, digital and hard copy with location map
Business cards with your capability statement
PHONES
1 x Incoming and 2 x Outgoing lines
Phone system — 2 portable handsets
If there are online billing opportunities systems like Hicaps/EFTPOS need a phone line. Can this be shared with another line or do you need separate line?
Hicaps machine
Answering service — noting that the phone messages are important
What is the phone number? You will need to order this.
IT
Internet connection
Laptops
Printer/photocopier/fax
Wireless connection
Website set-up
Practice software
Software licence required for paperless environment
Client data required for data conversion
Portable device to run software from treatment room

KEY SET-UP AREAS
PRACTICE FIT-OUT
Desk & typing chair for reception
Desk for treatment room
Reception chairs
Reception table for resources
Electrical beds
Stools
Storage unit for equipment
Exercise balls and equipment racks
Storage unit for client personal effects
Hand paper towel dispenser & towel for toilet & sinks
Filing cabinet
Stock display cabinet
Storage unit
Music system
Coffee cups, spoons, plates, glasses, knives & forks
Bar fridge, kettle
SPECIALIST EQUIPMENT
Purchased or obtained secondhand and re-located by removalist
Set date for equipment delivery
Extra equipment required — detailed
Real Time Ultrasound to be considered

KEY SET-UP AREAS
Reformers, gym equipment, ice machine etc
Mirrors
Gym floor and equipment
Specialist equipment such as VO2 max and spirometry
CONSUMABLE & RETAIL STOCK
Hand sanitiser
Paper towel
Toilet paper
Liquid cleaner for equipment
Plastic cups for water dispenser
Wipes
Strapping tapes
Fixomull
Premax
Scissors
Theratubing
Handigrip bandaging
Retail — Pilates gripper socks, spikey balls, moveinsit, soft balls
Tea & Coffee
Acupuncture needles
Surgical gloves
Mediswabs

KEY SET-UP AREAS
STATIONERY
Letterhead
Envelopes
Stamps
Stamp with Practice Address for mail
Stamps for practitioners
Pens, sticky tape, hole punch, stapler calculator, black marker
Manilla Folders for patient files
Clips for files
Clinical note paper, computer terminals
Brochure holder for practice brochure
Business card holders
Sticky notes
A4 plain paper reams
Spare printer cartridge
OTHER
Practice Bank Account setup — separate bank account for ease of operation
Finalise lease, add details, etc. All utilities/outgoings should be via centre
Agree to move in / start-up date — when can we get access?
Agree to business name and Register

KEY SET-UP AREAS
Get ABN or ACN or other government- or tax-required numbers/registrations
Set a budget for coming year
Builder/fit out company to build the rooms/ erect walls required
All client payments to be made via online or on site via credit card
Separate time sheet for staff & prac. business-related hours
New Provider Numbers to be applied for from HIC
Registration of Practitioners with Hicaps
Paper rolls for Hicaps machine
Digital Yellow Pages entries
Medical Waste container for sharps
Wall posters/art
Drinking water unit
Sanitary bins
Anatomy Models
Postal Box for mail or is delivery to practice address possible?
Designate admin person to process reports (weekly KPIs, commercial KPIs, EOM, practitioner pays, outstanding debt, accounts payable, order stock & stationery,
Linen - sheets, towels, slips, gowns Kylie purchase & wash

KEY SET-UP AREAS
Cleaner to be engaged
Vaccum cleaner to be purchased
Security system required?? Will depend on the facility
Access to premises — door open at all times. Do we need key out of hours?
MARKETING
Letter & brochure to known potential clients
Letter to Referrers on relocation
Briefing for Receptionists & script
News added to websites
Insert into Practice News update
Explore if there is a marketing brochure that could be shared with others

The above checklist is very detailed and provides the 'micro tasks' needed to be done to start your greenfield business. I will now deal with the more 'macro tasks' under the following headings: Branding, The Premises, The Fit-Out, Equipment, Colour Scheme, Signage, Systems and Policies, Pricing, Supply-Driven Demand, and Your Business Opening!

Branding

What will your business be named? What is the look and feel you want to have that will express the vision you have created? My advice regarding the name you choose is that the name should be able to tell people what you do, hopefully where you are, and still have some personality that will help people remember your business. As an example, when I was managing the LifeCare business, the format was to have the word LifeCare (with a capital L and C) to emphasise the notion that LifeCare provided care for your life journey in health, then the suburb name, and finally the key service provided, namely: Physio, Sports Medicine, Podiatry and so on.

Once you have a name, then think about a logo. This is a really hard task and you will likely need some professional assistance. Many marketing companies are able to do this for you, but they will ask you many questions to assist them with the logo and brand development. It is a good idea to have the creative people not only produce the logo but apply it to business cards, a web page, digital assets, letterhead and so on. It will not cost much more to get these important branding elements as part of the quotation for the work. Simple things like not having too many colours in the logo (two colour is best) are important as well and will save cost in the long term. Even in a paperless practice you will still need paper so do not see the above as unnecessary. A good logo will usually include your name, have a visual element and have some sort of capability statement to accompany. Examples of this might be "Committed to Service" or "Caring for our Community". By having a capability statement you are able to convey some of your vision to your potential clients and referrers.

The social media space is now an accepted part of any business branding. This means that you need to have some presence with the current digital vehicles that are available. It is not worth naming them all at the risk of them not being with us next year! I can advise that Facebook is a good idea for the business, as it will inform your community of your work and LinkedIn is important for having a presence in the professional community. Social media can also be a good place to advertise. Personal branding is another aspect of social media to consider. Once again, gaining some external advice may save you time and assist you to obtain a more professional look and feel for you and your business.

The Premises

The location has been chosen and you have decided to take on a lease. The agent can help ensure you have the correct permits and so on. Before you sign any lease, make sure the signing is conditional upon having the appropriate paperwork. Make sure you understand that you will pay a base rent for the space and then, more than likely, variable outgoings like rates, water, body corporate and so on. Such outgoings can cost up to 25% on top of the lease, so be warned. Once you know this, you can work out the gross rent that you will be paying annually. Working out how much you pay per square metre of space is important because when you start your business you may not utilise every square metre and knowing the cost of that unused space will motivate you to make sure you use it. Rent is one of the three main costs of running a professional practice after practitioner costs and then admin staff costs. The rent should ultimately be no more than 8% of the total billings you budget to make in the practice.

The Fit-Out

Creating a space that enables you to operate a good practice is always a challenge. The fit-out should allow for easy and logical client flow, meet the needs of the office staff, enable practitioners to provide optimum delivery of their service, and be comfortable and inviting for your clients. I advise the best way to achieve the above is to have a large piece of paper or computer image that is to scale and can be easily drawn upon. Even if you decide to engage a designer to assist with drawings for your builder or office fit-out company, it is important to make sure you have made some drawings of your own.

Ideally, draw to scale so that you can more easily picture where each area will be. The shape of your available space will dictate this, as will how you envisage the best flow for your clients. It sometimes helps to lay the real furniture and equipment out on any comparable floor space to get a visual of how the space will work.

Once done, you can take this drawing to a builder/

designer who can work with you to tidy it up! This process will also inform where you need to create fixed walls because you will want as much open space as you can get to provide a nice ambience for everyone to work in. The one area to pay extra attention to is the reception area. This is where you will display information for your clients about your people and what you offer, and it should also be somewhere they feel comfortable sitting. Consequently, the furniture you have and the look and feel of the reception bench/desk is also critical.

The scale picture below is the fit-out we used at the Bali Sports Medicine Clinic I have mentioned previously. This clinic was located in a hospital, and we had 75 square metres in which to create the practice fit-out.

The fit-out area included the following:
- two treatment rooms that measured around 2.5 x 3.6 sq m
- a consulting room of 17 sq m
- a space for reception and office and waiting area that was circa 20 sq m
- an open space that could be used for a gym or class or meeting area of 28 sq m
- storage of 2 sq m

This example is of a particularly small area but demonstrates how such a space can be used to operate a small business.

Figure 13: Practice Floor Plan — Bali Sports Medicine Clinic

Equipment

The type of practice you wish to operate will determine the equipment you will need. Rather than detail an endless list, I thought it useful to provide comments on the more generic items you will need. It may also be useful for you to divide the needs into what will be required in the following areas:

Administrative Areas

A statement can be made with an attractive yet functional reception bench/counter. Try and think about the height of the counter for both clerical staff and clients, how you will display your logo either behind reception or indeed on the front of the counter, and the dimensions of the counter so that staff can be easily accommodated behind the counter. Other furniture such as clerical seating, client seating, office desks, and so on, is a matter of taste in which you should considering the impact you wish to make on your clients. Tired and cheap items may be the wrong type of image you wish to convey. Many smaller items are required for a functional office and can be accessed at many stores or suppliers. Information technology is a difficult topic to be too prescriptive about due to the rapid change in this area. Suffice to say that you will need to have a computerised system if you wish to be part of the healthcare system into the future. Choosing the right hardware and software is a minefield and I suggest you liaise with a technology partner to assist you and maybe even consider having a contract with such a company to assist you into the future.

Treatment Areas

Equipping your treatment rooms to the standard you want is important. These days clients expect the plinths to be able to move up and down and have movable components for comfort and practicality. Invest in quality items. Having adequate shelving in the treatment room is also essential to stop you moving in and out of the room during treatment.

Open Areas

Ideally, you will have a space that can be used for multiple purposes. If you anticipate that you will gain referrals or business that requires your clients to do functional activities and exercise regimes in the practice, then this will direct the equipment you will need, e.g. bikes, weight machines, steps, and so on. Make sure you have some solid walls to attach exercise apparatus to and that you have several power points in the space, should you need any power. Consider not just the size of the space but the location of the space in the clinic if you plan to have group classes for Pilates or general exercise classes, or counselling groups, and if specialised equipment is needed, including treadmills, video feedback screens or cameras and so on.

Common and Utility Areas

Having an accessible bathroom will be important for your clients. Storage with shelving is very important and should be located in an appropriate place. Some sort of small kitchen/staff rest area will add to your culture. Similar items like drink coolers and coffee machines will do the same sort of thing. How you create a great environment in your practice is an area where you can add your personality and flair.

Colour Scheme

It is worthwhile creating a colour scheme for your practice. The colour scheme should start with your stationery and carry to a feature wall of the same colour and furniture to match. A designer can assist you here to get the look and feel that matches your practice and introduces a bit of personality to your premises.

Signage

External signage should be clear and uncluttered. Most signage companies will assist you by taking photos of the proposed signage and place the images on a digital image of your location/s so that you can see what the end product will look like. Ideally, the look of the external signage will match the look internally and match the colour scheme of the media you use in the practice. If you develop resources for clients, make sure they also carry the colour and look you want so that your clients will be constantly reminded of your business.

Systems and Policies

I do not intend to detail a fully comprehensive list of the systems and policies you may need in your business, but please consider the lists below and think about what you will need. Professional associations have resources to assist you with the systems and policies you will need, so ask your professional association for help.

Systems

- Internal Communications
- Billing/Receipting
- Appointments
- Item codes
- Debt control
- Ordering and stock
- Maintenance
- Housekeeping — security, linen, cleaning
- Telehealth — 2% of business is now with online telehealth and this is growing
- Virus (Covid) considerations, social distance, sanitiser. No magazines, so consider free Wi-Fi, TV or other items as an opportunity.

Policies

- Occupational Health and Safety
- Sexual Harassment
- Discrimination, risk in general
- Return to work
- Emergency/crisis plan — fire, bomb and so on
- Privacy

Pricing

There are many schools of thought about the fees to charge. By performing a competitor analysis and knowing what your professional association recommends regarding fee setting, you will gain insight into the fees you should charge when you commence practice. Price increases will become important and some of the comments below may be useful.

- If no one is complaining, then the price must be too low — this is strictly true because research shows that around 20% of clients complain about prices. Just make sure that you are very clear that you are aware of the comments being made.
- Put your prices up every six months — not a strict rule but the best times to increase prices are at the start of the financial and calendar years.
- Never price your service higher than your competitors — this depends on the quality of your service, facilities and people. Comparing different clinics to yours will help you know if what you have to offer is better and hence your prices can reflect that.
- Display discreet notices of your prices — it is important to make your clients aware of price and of price increases, but to advertise it with prominent posters and signs may make clients focus on just that and not the service you offer. Placing discreet signs at reception that say, "Our fees are in line with the recommendations of our professional body," or "In the interest of continuing to provide you with

excellent services, we have increased our prices to cover practice expenses."

- You must leave the price the same for current clients — with very good clients who will soon complete their treatment, this may help but it may be better to provide a few weeks' notice of a price increase and then apply that increase to all patients.
- If you are fully busy, you should put the prices up — certainly if your demand exceeds supply this is a potent consideration (more on supply and demand to follow).
- Increasing prices is three times more effective than increasing volume — research shows this to be true. Keeping pricing low to increase volume will mean you have many low-paying clients and hence more to manage.

Supply-Driven Demand

When we speak of supply-driven demand in health environments, it is important to identify what is supply and what is demand. In your clinic you 'supply' clinicians to see patients. Patients come to you and create a demand for the services you supply. One hopes, ideally, that you have enough demand to satisfy supply or vice versa. When this equation is out of balance, you need to address the imbalance. Let us look at some examples to illustrate this discussion and enable you to apply this in your business:

Supply Exceeds Demand

In this situation the power is with the patient. You have too many therapists' hours for the current demand. So you need to stimulate demand with special offers, diversification of your services and good old-fashioned relationship marketing to referrers or even lower your prices (although this often doesn't help and is a sign that your business is failing). Alternatively, you could reduce supply by decreasing hours available and stimulate demand as you have fewer vacancies. I recommend you retain supply until you have implemented your strategies to increase demand.

Supply Meets Demand

Although this may look good, as you have a balance, in reality you lack capacity to grow your business. In this example you should: review your product and look to diversify, watch trends with your opposition to ensure your price is still competitive (perform a competitor analysis as mentioned earlier by ringing like businesses near you), and continue your promotions. We advocate increasing supply as this will improve availability and you should work at being 80% busy as this will always allow growth.

Demand Exceeds Supply

Review your product in this instance and extend hours of consulting, promote value-adds, such as other services.

Increase your price and make sure the money you spend on promotions is low. This scenario needs addressing or else you may lose clients to other businesses. You need to act quickly and recreate a better balance in the supply-demand equation. In this example *you* have the power, not the patient, but this will not last if you do not act to redress the imbalance because patients will leave if waiting times balloon out.

Your Business Opening!

You can be creative when opening a new business. Local media, clubs, other businesses, councils and so forth are always looking for ways to support local business, so try to see what sort of assistance and publicity you may be able to attract. Family and friends should help provide a crowd and the provision of a tour and some refreshments at the opening is a must.

Setting up a greenfield business may all sound daunting, but it is important to look ahead beyond the work I've outlined above. It is important to consider your personal aspirations. Where do you want to be in 1, 2, 5 ,10 and 20 years? Think about where you 'see' yourself in five years, what will it look and feel like? How do you wish others to see you in five years? If enough consideration is given to deeply looking into these questions, much heartache can be avoided. It may help you to decide on the need to take on a partner, for instance.

As I mentioned in Section 2.4, you should always start a major and complex process with a clear vision of the final goal you aim to achieve. This applies as much to where you want the practice to get to, as to where you as an individual want to be, including how you may eventually exit the business. It will provide you with many ideas about how to create a personal mission statement that covers the direction you wish to head in your own life.

3.2.3 Growing Your Business

You have commenced your new business and now the fun begins of steadily gaining more and more patients and referrers.

If you have been practising elsewhere and now own your list, then it is likely that patients you have seen will want to follow you to your new business. I have experienced practitioners moving on from the businesses I have operated over the years, and my experience is that up to half the patients whom the practitioner saw will follow that practitioner. It has been my policy to instruct reception and admin staff that should a patient ask to see said practitioner when that person has left, that they offer an appointment with another practitioner, but if the patient insists, then to provide the details of where that practitioner is now working.

I have also assisted practitioners to be part of the establishment of a new business with them as equity partners. I recall a specific example when we decided to develop a rehab Pilates clinic nearby. The potential partner was working with us and was already seeing rehab Pilates patients there and was able to 'bring' those patient billings to the new practice, which gave us an immediate head start with patients attending from day one.

I will now discuss growing your business under the following headings: Finding New Patients, Communication, Referrer Relationships, Strategic Relationships, Health Industry Referrers, and MK's 19 Laws of Growth.

Finding New Patients

The difference for you now that you are developing a business is that not only do you need to find new patients for yourself, but also to find new patients for the practice, assuming you will have others working in your business who may be from different disciplines. The principles I spoke about in Stage Two will hold you in good stead. I will highlight some activities you can undertake to attract more referrers and more patients by word-of-mouth:

Communication

Developing different types of communications using both digital strategies and paper-based marketing will mean optimisation resources are required. Using social media is one method and either engaging a consultant or learning yourself to do search-engine marketing and then optimisation is a proven activity to get messages to your potential patients. Having a regular e-newsletter sent to your current and developing database can also be effective. Being creative with messaging and employing the SUCCES 'made-to-stick' approach to messages, which I mentioned in Stage Two, should yield good results. Regular communication with your current patients with follow-ups, contacting them a month after discharge to check on them, and special promotions and offers like discounts for referring a friend, or a massage voucher for a client who refers multiple friends are useful examples to adopt.

Referrer Relationships

I detailed this activity in Stage Two. I raise it again because you will need to work harder to develop even more referrers and incentivise those who work with you to also develop these relationships.

Strategic Relationships

Local clubs, businesses and schools are examples of possible referrers with whom it is worth you taking a more strategic approach.

Health Industry Referrers

In this example, you should build a database of medical specialists and GP's who could refer to you either because you know them or they are nearby or you know their reputation as great clinicians.

MK's 19 Laws of Growth

Growing is like climbing a ladder: step-by-step until you reach the top. Over many years of experience, I have developed a number of ideas and received constructive feedback on them, which I have now dubbed 'MK's Laws of Growth':

Steps 1–5

- Know who referred and how every new patient is referred to you.
- Keep a record of all referrers weekly.
- Persist when trying to gain a new referrer. It may take six encounters to start referrals flowing.
- Contact new referrals the same day by phone or letter. Always ask: "Were you referred today?" and, if no, then "How did you hear about us?"
- Satisfy your patient's needs beyond their expectations. Ask them about the things that are important to them and keep that detail on file — birthday, anniversary and so on. This will demonstrate that you care.

Step 6

Devise a written marketing plan for the practitioners and the business that sets out:
- How many new patients per month you wish to see.
- What level of gross billings you wish to generate each month.
- What you want your fees to be.
- A list of your current referrers and your proposed referrers that you will target (list in categories and frequency).
- Establish the preferred communication channel for each referrer, e.g. letter, visit, phone call and so on.
- Measure and record their referral habits and keep a record of your contacts with them.
- Trends in referrals, i.e. time of year, patient type and/or condition and keep this detail on file and so on.

Steps 7–14

- Run to time and set the patients' expectations.
- Put in place systems in case you run late, e.g. text to advise next patient(s) that you're running 10 minutes late.
- Understand the importance of the placebo effect. Examples include your smile, greeting and good presentation of your treatment area.
- Create the availability to see a referred patient

- as soon as the referrer wishes them to be seen. Remember to liaise with reception.
- Use your initiative when not busy to nurture your referrers with good communications.
- Analyse your new patients monthly. You should know what happened to each and every one of them — do you?
- Develop your personal USP that you can use to market to new referrers.
- Remember the three A's discussed in Stage One: Availability, Affability and Ability.

Steps 15–19

- Create a database of referrers in your area who work in large practices. Offer to present a summary on a diagnosis about a patient that you have co-managed with a GP.
- Follow up all patients that cancel or do not show.
- When you discharge a patient, tell them you will ring them in two weeks to check on their progress. They will then expect your call and, if they are having any difficulties, they may re-book.
- Once you have established a good rapport with your patients, talk to them about their networks and they may provide you with leads
- The story of the 'hook'. The 19th MK Law is worth elaborating upon. One of my previous equity

partners was a very well-qualified, competent and extremely popular practitioner. He advised me that when he watched a surgeon operate on ankle problems, the surgeon used a special stirrup cuff to distract the ankle joint when doing arthroscopy. The equity partner advised the surgeon that he also used such a distraction cuff when mobilising stiff ankle joints to gain the joints' separation. From that day on, the surgeon sent his used cuffs to the practitioner. The cuff was a 'hook' that helped the surgeon remember the practitioner who continued to receive many referrals from the surgeon.

Some of the above 'Laws' are a repeat from Stage Two, but I wanted to display them together to assist you to not only use them in your business but teach others to do so. See if you can add your own Laws! A final comment about growing your business is to remember that you need to work *on* your business for the business to grow, and not just *in* the business of seeing your own patients. This may not be comfortable but is necessary.

3.2.4 Managing the Business

Now that your business is open, you can move forward to operate and work towards the vision you have for the business. There are always many activities to attend to and I will address the key elements under the following headings: The Facility, Recruiting and Managing Staff and Practitioners, Retention and Equity Participation, Performance Leadership, Measures of Business Performance, Benchmarks, Reporting, Risk Management, Leadership, and Succession Planning.

The Facility

Although your facility will be sparkling and new (we hope) there is always maintenance and ways in which you can add to and improve your facility. It is good to have a monthly review of the facility to make sure that any wear and tear is being managed. You will also find as you grow there will be the need to add equipment to keep your business current. Your staff and practitioners will make suggestions because you will have an empowered work environment. I talked about such environments in Stage Two and it is important that your people feel supported and that their suggestions are heard and, within reason, acted upon.

Recruiting and Managing Staff and Practitioners

If you have opened, it is presumed that you already have some staff and also some practitioners to work and grow the business. I will discuss this area under the following headings: Recruitment, Induction, Training, Mentoring, Retention and Equity Participation, and Performance Leadership.

Recruitment

Recruiting the right person in the right place, right now is the challenge you face. Legendary car salesman RH Grant once said: "When you hire people who are smarter than you are, you prove you are smarter than they are." Start by identifying what you are looking for. The key to making a wise decision is to consider the long-term benefit versus the short-term cost. Try to look behind each person's CV to interests, character traits, community engagement, and so on. The main elements of the person's CV may appear shiny and fit with your requirements, but by asking some probing questions you can test the resolve of the applicant. A good example might be to ask what opinion they have about the future of the health industry or about new trends in their discipline. Such questions will test the depth of their knowledge further.

Induction

Induction is the absolute key because how your new staff member starts will often determine how it may end. This means that by having good induction procedures you are ensuring that the ongoing engagement of the staff member will be successful. I suggest having an initial chat some days before the start date, just to touch base and create a sense of readiness and excitement. If you have written procedures, policies and manuals that your practice has created, be aware of these and use them in the process.

Creating an induction checklist will help keep you on track and can be used for all induction. Make sure you clarify mutual expectations about important matters of operation. Such things include fees, how appointments are made and managed, the need for the practitioner to market themselves, when and how reviews will happen, who is there to support and so on. As part of the induction, introduce them to the key people in the business and walk around the location with them answering any questions and queries raised by the inductee.

Training

As part of training you should consider developing online and hard copy teaching resources and keep these in a library. It is also good to subscribe to useful journals and consider a journal club as an additional resource. Assist your new staff with practical on-the-job experience and help them plan their time and develop objectives that will further their clinical excellence and commercial success. The first few weeks are crucial to assist them to feel comfortable and welcome. Plan and use that time wisely. Add value by teaching them time management and show them the time management matrix in Figure 4. Be effective and efficient with your training and explain the difference between these two modes of working — don't interchange these.

Mentoring

I have discussed the importance and need for mentoring throughout this book. All staff and practitioners come with some strengths and skills to offer. A well-constructed and thought-out mentoring program should enhance these skills and assist in the development of complementary and new skills. In addition, providing this mentoring will ensure that your people see that your business is forward thinking and has a genuine desire to assist with their career development and learning. It will also ensure that your business is the place to be, and this should increase your staff and practitioner retention. It is also important that you, as the business owner, structure your time to develop the skills to mentor. Mentoring helps establish your leadership credentials but, of course, you can't do it all, so contracting others with the right capabilities will assist your business to provide the best possible mentoring program.

Retention and Equity Participation

Staff retention in a business is important as staff turnover is a cost in time and money as you need to re-teach and induct people constantly. Set some measures for retention. Annual retention of more than 80% across your entire staff is a good place to start. When I worked at LifeCare we conducted a four-year mentoring program. Retention improved from 70% to 90% for those persons that followed the mentoring to the letter. Mentoring is a good way to improve retention.

New staff and practitioners often come from your networks and word-of-mouth rather than from advertising, so be sure to focus on developing networks in your professional communities. Becoming a destination of choice where staff and practitioners cannot get better support elsewhere will assist your retention.

Creating a positive environment with empowerment, sufficient challenges, good internal communication, where commitments are met, where demonstrating integrity is a value, and mentoring and teaching are important will all help with retention. It is also good to have career options for your people. Demonstrate to them how they can develop with you and involve them in aspects of the business and allow and foster their contribution.

A great way to achieve the above, alongside potentially driving business growth, is through equity participation. That is, selling some of the equity in your business to a practitioner. Essentially, this is rewarding great performance whilst ensuring that the practitioner continues to work alongside you. This is a big move and the items below will assist you to decide whether this will work for you.

How is the equity valued?
Usually, and as mentioned previously, this can be viewed as a multiple of profit (see Section 3.2.1 and EBITDA calculations), and the multiple will vary depending on the

value the practitioner has already provided to the goodwill of the business.

Is the practitioner ready?
This aspect is usually difficult to assess accurately. In addition, I will always consider the questions outlined below.

Is the owner ready?
Consider whether you need extra help to spread the load or want to increase the growth of the business.

How much equity should be sold?
I look firstly at 10% as a start, with the promise of more equity once both parties see the value and show their capacity to work together as partners in the business.

Will selling equity lock in the practitioner for the owner to seek new opportunities without having to worry about the business operation?

Hopefully, in time, this is what will happen: if you mentor the practitioner well and involve them in important decision-making, then this should allow you to step back and be able to seek new opportunities.

What structure should be considered?
This depends on the current structure you have. I do prefer a unit trust structure, but suggest you take legal

advice in this instance. A unit trust is an unincorporated structure that allows investors to hold equity in the business, and when profits are made, they go straight to individual unit owners instead of reinvesting them back into the business.

Once you have considered the above items and are convinced that a practitioner will add value beyond providing competent service and has shown the capacity to grow their list, then they should be considered for the offer of equity.

The models for equity participation can take several forms:

1) a small percentage of the ownership

2) deciding to sell all the business equity to them

3) offering equity in a new business that you are considering opening

Options one and two are the traditional means of seeing equity taken up by practitioners. The first consideration to address is who in your staff qualifies? There are a number of factors that will help you here. Firstly, does the practitioner have access to capital? This may not matter, but having options in this instance may make the process more achievable (this is not essential as vendor finance is an option). Secondly, is the practitioner committed to the business and current role they occupy? Thirdly, do they spend a significant amount of time (75% or more) at the business and have they provided a number of years of service? Fourthly, have they shown an ability to assist the business to grow? Fifthly, have you observed any special talents they offer such as education officer, great mentor, proven ability to increase business billings, and so on? These talents are important and they demonstrate how the practitioner can add value as an equity holder. Sixthly, did you set goals for them and their career that they have achieved?

Timeframes will also need to be set once the practitioner has been approached with the opportunity. A likely timeframe will be between 90 and 120 days.

Option three is ideal if you are in the position of looking to grow your business and cannot spend as much of your time at the new business and need an extra leadership resource. In this circumstance, it is logical to offer equity where the practitioner shares the costs of establishment, rather than pays any premium for business ownership. For example, if the cost to establish is $30K and they wish to be a 20% equity holder, then they would pay $6K (20% of the $30K). It is also important to ensure the practitioner understands that in start-up businesses it will usually take three years to see any profit.

Ultimately, practitioner equity participation in your

business benefits both you, the owner, and the practitioner. It is a great investment and one that both owners and practitioners can influence and have control over, unlike some other investment categories, for example, shares and property. For the business owner, having the input of new ideas will help reshape, improve and continue the business's success. For the practitioner, the whole process will create enormous job satisfaction. Business growth is an exciting thing to create. Seeing the KPI's reached, the business achieves new targets, and exploring new markets is something to watch and enjoy and will justify the extra work it might place on both the new equity holder and the business owner.

Performance Leadership

Reviewing performance used to be called 'performance management'. As the aim of a review is to improve performance, I prefer to call the process 'performance leadership'. There is a structure to this that I have used satisfactorily for many years. This involves setting a plan with clear objective measures up front (KPI's)! This approach involves reviews of these KPI's either monthly, quarterly or annually. I prefer to do different levels of reviews quarterly. Achievement or not of KPI's will effectively score the review. A managing director I worked with in the corporate environment used to say that: "The score at the end of the game determines who wins the game."

Performance leadership should also assist in good relationship development and not be seen as a chore or a stressful activity.

There are three distinct levels of performance leadership:

1) Feedback

2) Assessment

3) Review

1. Feedback

Provide feedback regularly and often. Try to provide such feedback in the first person, e.g. "I have noticed..." It should be based on a clear, factual and objective observation of performance.

Always begin with a positive. It is easy to be seen as nit-picking, so I always make a positive observation in some way, even if I need to provide something that may not be seen as positive. For example, let them know how pleased you are that they are punctual or that you heard them say something really good to a patient, or that the other staff really enjoy having them in the business. The skill is to open the communication in a positive manner before delivering more critical feedback. Ensure the feedback is non-judgemental and refer to what you have observed rather than what you might have heard. Hopefully, what you say will invite a response from your staff or practitioners.

2. Assessment

Assessment is a more formal approach to performance leadership. This is best to perform once you have provided feedback, but have noticed the non-desirable behaviour hasn't changed. An example of such behaviours may be that the language they are using with patients is overly friendly, or other staff may have mentioned that they were hearing feedback from patients that the attitude of the practitioner is indifferent to the person being treated. Provide objective and non-judgemental feedback in a formal setting that invites a response and hopefully discussion. Go into detail regarding why an action is appropriate/inappropriate and offer suggestions or provide directions or alternative actions if required. Providing resources to assist new behaviour, e.g. articles, some training or role-playing to provide a personal demonstration of the desired action can work well. In role-play you will take the position of the patient and provide responses to the practitioner that highlight the issues at hand and then model the correct responses/behaviour.

3. Review

A formal review should be scheduled annually or biannually, rather than performed in the moment like feedback or assessment. To gain the best outcome, preparation is required by both parties. Schedule the time for the review and advise the format the review will take. This may involve completion of a form that details each area of performance the review will cover, such as attitude, actual review of agreed KPI's, how the person works in a team, and so on. The review should be documented and use both the agreed quantitative KPI's and qualitative measurements such as their attitude and so on. Once completed, the review documents should be signed off by both parties.

Measures of Business Performance

Any measures that you create should be meaningful to you and also highlight important aspects of the business. If you create too many key measures, you will get lost reviewing them. I recommend that you have no more than five measures for the different aspects of the business, like finance performance, business culture, staff performance, a referrer database, annual growth measures as examples. Create clear objectives for these key areas. Have three to five methods of achieving the objective and have measures that can be assessed with either a yes or no answer.

An example is provided below.

> **Area: Finance Performance**
>
> **Key Objective:** Achieve a break-even target (i.e. expenses and income are even) for the practice by the end of the second year of operation.
>
> **Method of achieving this objective:** Have enough referrers to achieve enough client visits to meet billing targets.
>
> **KPI:** Have 20 referrers referring more than one client per month so that we see 80 patients per week within 3 months of starting the operation.

You will note here that the above example meets the criteria of being a SMART (Specific, Measurable, Achievable, Realistic and Timely) objective. The practice knows they need a certain number of referrers and clients within a timeframe. It is also clear enough that others can buy into your plan.

Benchmarks

In many industries there are benchmarks that act as a guide to what certain costs should be as a proportion of total costs. Such benchmarks assist greatly with cost management and act as a guide for you in your business. To give you some assistance, I have compiled indicative percentages of total business gross costs to aim for:

- 45% Cost of practitioners

- 12% Staff
- 10% Premises
- 8% General and administration expenses, like printing and stationary, banking, etc
- 2.5% Public relations and marketing
- 2.5% Communications technology
- 2.5% Other

This leaves 18.5% as your sustainable earnings. The cost of your premises is one of the key metrics to establish to achieve sustainable earnings, combined with the cost of staff and practitioners.

Reporting

Setting up regular reporting of progress is essential to know how your business is travelling at key time points. Two important reports that should be performed with your accountant are monthly profit and loss statements, and the annual budget that covers the projected income and expenditure for the coming year. The third important report is your weekly KPI report:

In the table spread across the following four pages (192-195) there are some abbreviated examples of the sort of weekly data that will help you keep track of the performance of many key measures. The examples are taken from a multidisciplinary business that we operated at LifeCare. Note that there are a number of 'services' in such a business. The table is indicative and is a snapshot of a few weeks in a calendar year. This table also includes what we call 'working capital'. Working capital is money you are creating to operate the business because not all monies are collected at the time of service, for instance, delivery debt can be accumulated.

The next table, in Figure 15, is lifted from the table in Figure 14. The measures indicate what we thought were the most important ratios for the business weekly.

The first three measures are derived from three pieces of information: Hours weekly for staff and practitioners, Weekly gross billings, and Weekly patient numbers.

Figure 15. Measures of Staff Performance

Ratios:							
Revenue per Clinician Hour	$89.77	$64.01	$85.75	$70.79	$62.69	$68.86	*$72.32*
Patients per Clinician Hour	2.67	1.80	2.63	1.84	1.65	1.98	*2.04*
Revenue per patient	$33.66	$35.50	$32.55	$38.39	$37.89	$34.79	*$35.44*
Patient cost to Serve	$16.01	$16.30	$14.07	$14.46	$17.05	$18.57	*$22.74*
Staff Hrs per Clinician Hour	0.70	0.49	0.63	0.44	0.49	0.56	*0.54*
Est wages costs as a % of billing	17%	16%	16%	13%	17%	18%	*16%*
Patient Mix							
Physio Patients	93%	93%	95%	94%	96%	97%	*95%*
Massage Patients	6%	6%	3%	5%	4%	3%	*4%*
Podiatry Patients	0%	0%	0%	0%	0%	0%	*1%*
Other Patients	0%	0%	0%	0%	0%	0%	*0%*

While working in practitioner networks, I designed a 'league table' of all practitioners based on the dollars per hour they generated in their practices. This process was considered quite controversial and 'all about money', until it became evident that those with the highest dollars generated per hour were also seen in the network as the most capable and highly regarded clinically. Which

Figure 14: Weekly KPI Report

KPI Report CONSOLIDATED					
		SNAPSHOT PERIOD			
Week No:		45	46	47	48
Week ended:		10/05/09	17/05/09	24/05/09	31/05/09
Key Value Drivers		Do not enter data in this section			
REVENUE					
Clinician Revenue\					
	Physiotherapy	24,639	25,954	25,311	23,688
	Podiatry				
	Pilates: Clinician Shared	2,401	2,174	2,698	2,560
	Sports Medicine				
	Other	775	591	527	735
	Total	27,815	28,719	28,536	26,984
Centre Billings					
	Pilates: Clinician Paid Hourly				
	Babyswim				
	Total	0	0	0	0
	TOTAL BILLINGS	27,815	28,719	28,536	26,984
PATIENT VOLUME					
	Physiotherapy	457	486	466	452
	Podiatry				
	Pilates	86	79	98	93
	Babyswim				
	Sports Medicine				
	Other	13	13	13	14
	TOTAL PATIENTS	556	578	577	559

49 07/06/09	50 14/06/09	51 21/06/09	52 28/06/09	Snapshot Period	52 YTD Weekly
				Average	Average
23,399	17,928	18,655	24,590	23,021	22,584
				0	0
2,262	2,139	2,074	2,139	2,306	1,737
				0	0
319	291	398	1,243	610	835
25,979	20,358	21,127	27,972	25,936	25,156
				0	0
				0	0
0	0	0	0	0	0
25,979	20,358	21,127	27,972	25,936	25,156
429	337	346	456	429	424
				0	0
82	75	74	77	83	62
				0	0
				0	0
6	6	8	14	11	23
517	418	428	547	523	509

KPI Report CONSOLIDATED					
CLINICIAN HOURS					
Service & Facility Clinician Hours		223	227	217	219
Salary & Wage Clinician Hours		40	53	55	52
	TOTAL CLINICIAN HOURS	263	280	272	271
	Full-Time Equivalent Clinician Hours	9	9	9	9
PRODUCTIVE SUPPORT STAFF HOURS		181	180	186	182
	Sick Leave	0	0	7	0
WORKING CAPITAL					
	Debtors				
	Debtors — all				
	0 — 30 days	10,467	18,153	25,356	18,819
	31 — 60 days	26,240	19,955	13,988	19,016
	61 — 90 days	11,862	8,465	7,076	7,588
	90 + days	11,306	10,401	8,905	10,217
	Total Debtors	59,875	56,974	55,325	55,640
	Bad debts written off			65	
RATIOS					
	Billings per Clinician Hour	105.86	102.45	104.79	99.49
	Patients per Clinician hour	2.12	2.06	2.12	2.06
	Patients per Productive Support Staff hour	3.08	3.22	3.10	3.08
	Gross revenue per patient	50.03	49.69	49.46	48.27
	Support Staff Hours per Clinician Hour	0.69	0.64	0.68	0.67
	Days Outstanding	15.11	13.93	13.61	14.47

Leading Your List — Maximise Equity

204	153	172	220	205	194
51	46	57	56	51	49
255	199	229	276	256	243
9	7	8	9.2	9	8
177	161	163	174	175	173
0	0	0	3	1	0

10,771	14,561	22,822	29,781	18,841	
25,474	24,168	19,139	13,348	20,166	
12,994	5,700	4,955	2,117	7,595	
7,261	7,413	6,114	4,813	8,304	
56,500	51,842	53,030	50,059	54,906	
			0	33	9

101.78	102.30	92.16	101.26	101.39	103.33
2.03	2.10	1.87	1.98	2.04	2.09
2.93	2.60	2.62	3.14	2.98	2.94
50.25	48.70	49.36	51.14	49.64	49.42
0.69	0.81	0.71	0.63	0.69	0.71
15.27	17.87	17.62	12.56	14.86	0.00

reinforced that being clinical excellent leads to commercial success.

The points I am making is that the measures, ratios, benchmarks and reports you may implement must have relevance for your business. The format of the tables is also up to your preference. The main focus should be on being able to review performance on a timely basis to ensure your plans are on track.

Risk Management

In any business there are risks. How you identify the risks and then work to mitigate them will in large part determine your success in business.

Take action to ensure you deal with varied business risks. Some examples are:

- Compliance with regulations, such as current registration, accreditation, quality management, clinical regulation, policies regarding privacy, anti-discrimination, sexual harassment, bullying and so on.
- Trade practices, ACCC. Make sure you do not denigrate others who work in the industry in your promotions, or use advertising that is clear testimonial.
- Build good and sustainable relationships and have thorough internal communication processes like regular memos and staff meetings to identify and solve problems and deal with any complaints.
- Ensure you have occupational health and safety policies, and review such matters at least monthly.

- Adequate insurances, including public liability, professional indemnity, directors and officers, and so on.

Leadership

If you are providing leadership in your business, you should be performing three key roles:

1. Teaching

Teach at every opportunity to those you work with. Look to create both formal and informal opportunities to teach and encourage those who work with you to do likewise.

2. Communication

At all times make sure you are communicating with your team. The role of communication is to: inform, change attitude, direct action, resolve conflict, generate ideas and discuss issues. I suggest using various modes of communication because people might prefer to respond via different channels of communication. The different channels include: face-to-face, phone, teleconference, email and other business communications that can refer to websites and a range of resources. Be mindful to choose a channel that works for the person or team you are dealing with. I had a partner some years ago who was not as effective with face-to-face communication as he was with teleconferences. He created all of his meetings via teleconferences because his meetings face-to-face did not add value to his interactions.

3.   Planning

I have mentioned planning many times in this book. Having a plan makes it more likely that you will achieve the detail of the plan. In business, your team wants to know where the business is heading, what new activities you may be preparing, or new innovations you may bring to the business. Share your plans as much as you can without overloading your team.

Succession Planning

Having people working with you who are ready to step up and take on new roles, assist with growth and be a key part of your business's future can be addressed by succession planning.

Here are some brief points that you should consider with succession planning. It is never too early to be thinking of the future of your business.

- Start with the final goal/s in mind ... and recruit well.
- Understand what type of business you have and want, and what the values of your practice are. Review your structure, unit trust, partnership, profit share and equity options, as these elements often assist with planning to take on partners into your business.

- Have a defined mission and values to align you, the practice and your staff.
- Induct and train your people well, so they are ready to step up.
- Enable responsibility early to provide direction for your people and identify to them that they have a future with your business.
- Teach.
- Provide a golden handcuff. The idea of offering people the opportunity to become a partner with you was considered a golden handcuff. Something that would ensure that good people would not leave the business. This may be the case but is no guarantee. Best to provide such opportunities to those who ask for it and to those who show a strong willingness to contribute.
- Create options for people to expand into different roles like mentoring, marketing, and management and so on.

There will be practitioners who just want to see patients and develop their list without the expectation of being an equity partner or gaining a profit share. I think of Hayley when I discuss this. Hayley is a sports physio who works at a sports practice west of Melbourne. Hayley likes to work in elite sport and is busy. Hayley wants to go to elite events, as well as have the security of a business that supports her. She isn't interested in becoming an equity partner, even though she has the clinical excellence and commercial success to do so. This arrangement is mutually beneficial, and both the business and Hayley are thriving.

3.2.5 Long-Term Planning

It can be challenging to set plans for one, two, five and ten years mainly because such planning involves lifestyle elements, family responsibilities and career opportunities. For many years I have used two formal documents to assist practitioners: Achieving Your Career Objectives (Appendix 1) and Achieving Your Business Objectives (Appendix 2). These documents always contain a section about where a practitioner or business wished to be in two and five years. It was surprising how open practitioners were to advising us that they wished to marry, or they wished to buy a house, or go on a six-month holiday and so on. This openness enabled the business to assist them to achieve their long-term goals and to accommodate them within the business and create synergy with business goals.

I will now address some other important elements to consider with long-term planning under the following headings: Leveraging Time, Employing Others, Engaging Consultants, and Future Financial Needs.

Leveraging Time

Making a long-term plan is an effective way to continue a growth trajectory. Creating the time to do the planning is an exercise of efficiency and should be something you review and add to each year that you operate the business. Applying yourself to this task will decrease the risk of making decisions that aren't in the mid- and long-term interests of your people and your business. Your time is limited and considering what to do with the hours you have is a way of leveraging that time to best advantage.

Employing Others

As good and effective as you might be as an owner and business operator, there will be tasks that you can delegate to others. Leave behind the idea that "No one does it as well as I can, so don't bother employing others to help." This is an exercise in futility. Identify what you do well and want to continue to do, then assign a value to the other tasks you don't want to do, weighing them against the option of employing someone else to do that task. You may think this is taking income away from you and the business, but by careful delegation you should be able to see that you gain even better results than you might be able to, given the time you have.

Engaging Consultants

Having the ability and foresight to realise that you do not have every answer and the requisite knowledge of every aspect in your business is something to understand and act upon early in the operation of your business. Consultants will have specific skills you can access from time to time and even engaging such people to help with the development of a long-term plan is very important. I remember some years ago I had developed, with partners, five significant sports medicine practices in Melbourne. The partnership that we had developed had 13 equity partners from four different disciplines. The partnership eventually ran its course and we decided to engage a consultant who created the strategy of "Build to Sell". I will expand on this strategy in Stage Four but, in brief, over a four-year engagement, the consultant assisted our partnership to make some important changes to the businesses and ensure all partners were aligned with these new strategies, which led to a successful sale of the business.

Future Finance Needs

Long-term planning will identify what future you envision. You may want to move to larger premises or do a new fit-out or even buy another business. If you want to do any of these activities, you will need finance. Planning will assist you to understand the finance you need and how you plan to access that finance.

3.3   Why is Maximising Equity Important?

Now you have taken the step to develop your own business, either as a greenfield start-up or via the path of buying equity in an existing business, it is worth considering why maximising equity is important. My father was a specialist doctor working in obstetrics and gynaecology. He worked very hard at all times of the day and night delivering babies and caring for women's health. In those days there was no such thing as superannuation and also no training for professionals in business. My father never created a business. He had a practice that, at the end of his time, just dissipated and his patients went elsewhere. The only payment he received was from the sale of the small house that he operated his practice from.

There are other great benefits and challenges to having equity in a business, no matter what industry you may be involved in.

The Benefits

A great mentor of mine many years ago used to say:

"Michael, you can own property, shares, have fixed income in bank deposits, et cetera, but to own your own business is truly liberating, as you will have control over the asset which you do not have with other investment classes and the business will make money for you while you sleep."

This is a great sentiment but you need to ensure you don't become a slave to the business and that it does create passive income, which means that the earnings generated are not entirely from the work you have to do yourself. Operating a business can be very satisfying as you have created something that you can be proud of. Watching the business grow and seeing milestones achieved that you have planned for creates a sense of pride and joy. In your chosen profession others will see what you have done and this will bring new-found respect and even better connection with peers, which in turn helps the business to grow. As a business owner, you will have access to other business owners, and that camaraderie will be a source of new ideas and potential opportunities to expand your business. This can happen by establishing another business, merging with others, or having the opportunity to sell your investment in the years to come.

The Challenges

The concept of working "*on* your business, rather than *in* your business" is a common saying. As a practitioner, you will have been validated by seeing and helping your patients. This is a good thing, but you are now in a position to maximise your equity and hence cannot see every patient yourself. This can be a challenging change. You need to recruit others, to teach and mentor them to do what you have done. If you do this, you will be working *on* your business not *in* your business.

Developing new skills is sometimes confronting, particularly when you have never formally studied finance, marketing, strategy, people and culture. Understanding your limitations is important, as this will lead you to seek assistance from advisors, consultants or even to embark on extra study, like studying for an MBA. Do not be afraid, but embrace the learning of new skills just as you have to become clinically excellent and commercially successful as a practitioner. Management, strategy and commercial skills will all be necessary to make sure you continue building and growing your business. That is the challenge, so don't shy away from that challenge.

3.4 What Else Do I Need to Maximise Equity?

I have touched on many of these things, but in summary the need to develop and grow your business makes it necessary to expand your network of referrers, constantly improve your clinic and your processes, and continue recruiting and mentoring new people. To increase your business profile, lecturing widely and taking in students who are in training will help create greater profile and recognition for your business. Ensure you have a pipeline of practitioners from universities and schools that you can bring into your business as you grow. Aligning with these institutions and universities may also lead to joint research and the publishing of articles that will generate reputational advantages for your business. Working in sporting teams at elite and sub-elite levels creates networking and learning opportunities. Volunteering should also be a part of what you do and you will be seen as giving back to your profession, which engenders goodwill and will enhance your and your business's reputation.

Seeking out good mentors for yourself at this stage of your journey should continue. Remembering a good mentor for improving people and culture may be different to a finance mentor or a corporate consultant. Choose wisely and use word-of-mouth to identify such people. And don't be too quick to judge your mentor by their formal education. I have been working as a healthcare business consultant and find that — although I do not have formal finance, IT, or marketing training — because I have worked in the industry and operated businesses of many kinds and shapes that I can answer many of the questions practitioners and business owners have. In addition, I also have a network of other experts I can refer people to.

The process of building your business is an ongoing one. Someday, though, you will be looking to where the journey takes you next. I will now move to addressing the next stage of your journey.

4.0 STAGE FOUR

Selling Your List — Leverage Equity

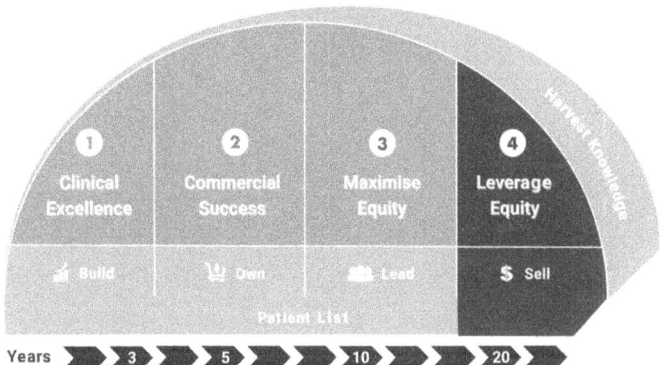

4.1 Who is Stage Four For?

Stage Four is the final stage of the practitioner's journey. If you have come this far, then you will realise that gaining clinical excellence, commercial success and developing your own business, or partnering with others in a business, has been the focus of your work and career. If you have read this far, you will now be looking to see if you can leverage the efforts, time and money you have applied to the three earlier stages. I have continued to use the metaphor of 'your list' and, at this stage, the list you have grown earlier in your practice has become part of the business you have developed and has become entwined with the practices of those who work with you. So, in a way the extended list is what holds the value for you in your business. Leveraging equity means that this asset you have developed, and the equity you hold in it, has value. Not just to you but potentially to others.

Stage Four will not be for everyone and not everyone will come to this point at the same time. I have identified several scenarios that better illustrate who this stage is for:

The Opportunist

Jack was approached to sell his business and realise the equity he had developed. He was not expecting this, as he was still thinking about what more he could do with the business and, in fact, had plans to do so. He had a tricky decision to make. The offer was more than he expected his business was worth but, if he sold, what would he then do with his time? The business was going well and growing steadily, and he had done the hard work to get there. So was it the right time to sell?

I have always said that one should start with a final goal in mind, and your exit should never be totally out of sight. Upon hard reflection, Jack decided to sell. He worked out with the interested purchaser how long he would stay at the business, what his role could be as the business ownership was transferred, and decided to use this time of handover to review his options post sale.

The Retiree

Stephen had operated his small business for 20 years. He wanted to unlock some money to use in preparation for his retirement and decided to make it known that he was looking to retire in the next few years. He had not 'had it' with operating his business; instead he wanted to stay involved by seeing the patients who had loyally helped him build his business. A new owner might bring new ideas and even more services and Stephen could play a role in providing stability while continuing to be part of the goodwill of the business. He didn't have to operate the business or make the decisions or build the systems. In short, worrying about the business could be transferred to another. Plus, Stephen was not ready to completely retire. It worked for him, and he continued in the role for two years post business sale and then retired to pursue his new life post work.

The Life Changer

Mary had worked fruitfully in her small business for many years, but had recently felt that something was missing. Her business was a solo affair with a couple of part-time practitioners. Mary worked in the local hospital as well, and she decided that when an offer came to buy her business, she would like to keep a few sessions with the new owners and continue her hospital work without the hassle of operating the business. Mary also had other changes in her life. She had a new partner and they wanted to build a small home in the surrounding hills and tend to the garden along with a small flock of goats they had acquired. A change of life had driven Mary to make this decision — not just a great financial offer, but the offer of new opportunities in her life.

The Corporate Opportunity

Phillip had worked very hard for more than 10 years. He was a go-getter. Starting with the purchase of a suburban business in the west of the city, he had gradually expanded and now owned four businesses within a 15-kilometre radius of the initial business. Business was good. He had good staff and practitioners were billing more than $2 million across the four businesses. Deep down, though, he felt ready for a new challenge. The allied health practice environment had seen the start of several corporate entities that were looking for investment-grade businesses to grow their networks. Phillip was ready for them and their offer. What attracted Phillip was the fact that the corporation was looking for managers to assist with their network growth. They wanted somebody who had shown the capacity to operate a small network of businesses, who was keen to develop new skills and had already started some postgraduate training in business management. Phillip sold his practices and looked forward to developing his skills with the corporate as a manager.

The corporate opportunity could also come through headhunting. The corporate identifies a business operator they like and offers to buy the business because they see this business operator and their business operation as a significant asset.

The Career Changer

I have seen practitioners who own their business decide that they need to pursue something different from operating a business. They often say it's a calling. For example, they want to teach full-time or to develop a career helping others run their businesses or to take on another challenge in a different industry. I will look at this type of change in the next section, as I know many people who have done this and it's always interesting and compelling to read their stories and see what's possible.

4.2   What is Leveraging Equity?

What do I mean when I talk of equity? In healthcare, equity can also describe something else altogether. The aim of healthcare equity is to ensure that everyone can access affordable, culturally competent health care regardless of:

- Race
- Ethnicity
- Age

- Ability
- Sex
- Gender identity or expression
- Sexual orientation
- Nationality
- Socioeconomic status
- Geographical location (i.e. rural or urban)

This is not the definition of equity I'm going to describe in this section, and I have touched on what it means earlier, but it may be worth detailing the meaning for you some more.

Equity is **the amount of money that a business's owner has put into it or owns.** On a balance sheet, the difference between liabilities and assets shows how much equity the business has. The value set by valuation experts or a purchaser is used to figure out the equity or business value.

Equity can be owned or built in a number of ways. You can own a home and the equity you have will be the dollar difference between what you owe the bank and what your property is valued at. Having shares in a company is another way you can have an equity share in a company. In a healthcare practice, your equity is the value that your business is worth based on the percentage of the shares/units in the business entity you own and the multiple of the profit that your business may be valued at. For example, you may own 25% of the equity and the profit/earnings are $100K a year. Your distribution would be 25% of $100K

= $25K; if the multiple used to value the equity by the purchaser is '4 x earnings', then your equity is worth 4 x $25K or $100K.

Equity is the ownership and value you have in your business. Hence you can share this with another by having them buy into your business. Leveraging your equity effectively is making sure that you get the best possible price for your business, should you decide to sell. There are a number of ways to sell this equity:

- Sell your practice outright to another healthcare practitioner.
- Be part of a management buyout, where those you work with in the practice buy your equity.
- Sell your practice to a corporate.

Alternatively, you could just walk away from your business when you have had enough, but for me that isn't an option.

There are a number of aspects to leveraging your equity that will operate to increase the value of your business before the sale and indeed help you make that sale. I will discuss this under four headings: Activities to Undertake to Leverage Equity, Defining your Business Assets for a Buyer, Valuing Equity, and Selling Equity.

4.2.1 Activities to Undertake to Leverage Equity

The following activities need to be considered under the following headings: Presentation, Premises and Equipment Leasing, Debts and Liabilities, Clean P&L, and Future Plans.

Presentation

How does your business look? The value of your practice will reside in the billings you generate and the profit you achieve, as we have discussed, but how the business presents is equally important. If your business looks tired — the floor surfaces are worn, equipment is outdated, waiting spaces are uninviting, and so on — then the appeal will be diminished to a potential purchaser. A purchaser will want to come into the practice and function at a high level from the outset. You will need to have others come and visit whom you trust and openly ask them what they think you could do, in a similar way to how one presents their house for sale. A part of presentation is how the space you have (which is an asset in the business) is utilised. I am often told: "We have extra space that we do not know what to do with." If you have under-utilised rooms and space that you thought you could use as a gym or for class activities or that one day you would rent out, then these issues need to be addressed before you sell.

Premises and Equipment Leasing

A purchaser will want to know that the lease for the premises is secure, and you have all appropriate permits to operate. Equipment service contracts should be up to date and performed as dictated by suppliers. The same applies to cleaning contracts. How you maintain your premises is very important to presentation, as we discussed above, and will add value to your business.

Debts and Liabilities

Most businesses try to have payments for services made at the time of treatment. If not, then you are accumulating debt, which needs to be followed up at a later date to ensure collection. Make sure you do not have high levels outstanding, e.g. greater than 5% of total billings. Liabilities outstanding might be related to the hot water service or air conditioning if it is continually breaking down and needs replacing. Other liabilities may include an audit by a compensable body or some insurer for bad practices. If such matters are relevant, then they must be disclosed.

Clean P&L

You will need assistance with the presentation of your accounts to a purchaser. It is important to not have home insurances in your business or a salary for your partner, who may not work with you. Unrelated superannuation payments should be separated from your business accounts. Also, car payments and payments for services that are not really part of the business are other matters that need addressing. I have seen such line items when deciphering a P&L statement, and they should be deleted and managed in your home accounts. These line items will not engender confidence in a purchaser.

Future Plans

Although a purchaser may not follow such plans, it is an asset to show that you have plans for the business. For example, a plan to target new referrers, or a plan for a strategic alliance with a large sport club, or a plan with a supplier to reduce your costs. These plans show you are actively operating the business and wish to see it improve further. Plans to expand and grow your staff can be seen as forward thinking and may show that there is room to grow the business when in the hands of the new owner.

4.2.2　Defining Your Business Assets for a Buyer

The following assets need to be defined for the buyer: The Business Billings, Business Structure, Your Client Database, Unique Factors, A Network, Specialty Referrers, and Good Business Systems.

The Business Billings

Having high billings, say greater than $1 million, is a good place to begin. If you are achieving a profit margin of 17% (hence a profit of $170K) then the value of your business will be a multiple of the $170K. If your billings are less than $1 million, then you may have other attractive aspects to entice a purchaser that are included below. If your business is more boutique, providing unique services from one or two rooms, it does not mean that you cannot sell, it just means that finding the right buyer may be more difficult.

Business Structure

Many purchasers are happy to buy your business operations but not the entities you have established to operate under. They want a clean purchase and structure when they start. So if they value your business, don't be surprised if they don't want to buy the company or trust you created when you established the business.

Your Client Database

Having a detailed loyal client database that can be accessed digitally is an asset. Good loyal clients come more often and refer others. When selling, a purchaser will want to be sure that those clients will continue to support the practice. Your clients will do this if they are made aware that things will not change too much and that you and your existing practitioners intend to stay for a period of time to ensure your clients' needs are met. How you communicate with your clients, if a sale is to occur, will need to be managed well. Good, open and timely messaging is essential.

Unique Factors

Your business may have services that are unique to your area or even to your city, e.g. specific equipment, a consulting service for trauma, a practitioner with special skills in manipulation or in treating specific populations like children. Such services, when marketed well, draw clients from near and far and are an asset to your business. Your business may be in a unique location which has easy access and a strong referral base, or be in an affluent area where you may be able to charge more for your services.

A Network of Businesses

Value will be created in the purchase of a single business. Clearly valuations will be higher if the purchaser has multiple businesses in a network to purchase. This is because having a network enables a purchaser to perhaps have control of the referrer base in a particular area or region. That said, purchasing a network of businesses is often beyond the purchasing power of an individual or younger person without significant financial resources.

Specialty Referrers

As touched on above, individual businesses can have value enhanced by providing some speciality service or having a significant referral base such as a professional sports team or particular testing or rehab equipment.

Good Business Systems

I detailed these systems in Stage Three of the journey, but to list them again, they are: ensuring you have staff contracts in place, ensuring you have a system for staff appraisals, ensuring there's a maintenance structure around your premises and equipment, ensuring you have a workplace health and safety system, ensuring you have a thorough induction procedure, alongside a practitioner and staff mentoring and training approach.

Ultimately, having good paperwork, thorough records and contracts in place is an asset, just as having other good systems is. If your contracts are up to date and have been legally created and monitored, they should be safely and confidentially filed away. As should positive staff annual appraisals that show that your people are content and have remained with you for years. This shows stability. Turnover of staff is a financial cost that is usually accompanied by leakage of patients who seek continuity in the practitioners they wish to see.

Defining the above systems for a buyer shows that the business is cared for and is running smoothly, without having attendant issues that will need to be addressed.

4.2.3 Valuing Equity

The next thing to consider is how do you set the value of your equity? The adage that "Something is only worth what someone is prepared and willing to pay" is a truism that applies to valuing your business.

The three matters to consider with the valuation for the purchaser are: Sustainable Profit, Physical Assets, and Goodwill.

Sustainable Profit

A purchaser will look for earnings (profit) that are consistent — not high one year, then low the next. Allowances were made for the Covid pandemic where practices 'normalise' their billings and profit to what is reasonably expected under the circumstances. This is acceptable in such cases. I used a scenario in the Business Billings paragraph above (under section 4.2.2) where a business was achieving a 17% profit margin. If, in this situation, you can demonstrate that for the past three years you have achieved this profit margin and your total business billings show gradual increases year on year, then this sustainable profit, from my experience, should prove very attractive to a buyer.

Physical Assets

Your business will have items of plant and equipment, stock, supplies and systems (namely computers) that will be considered a part of the purchase value. Some speciality items make up part of the plant and equipment and should be itemised clearly, and their value demonstrated by the income they produce as part of the services that utilise them. Some examples might be joint-strength testing equipment, rehabilitation equipment or other systems used for assessment or diagnosis. The look and feel of the business and the quality and currency of the fit-out are also recognised as having value. The above items will not usually be individually valued (other than the extra speciality equipment), but will contribute to the multiple of earnings (EBITDA) value, which I explained in Section 3.2.2. Such asset items may be the difference between a valuation of three-times earnings and up to five-times earnings. Therefore, it is worth making sure that you have reviewed and ensured that you emphasise how these assets add value to your business to the prospective purchaser.

Goodwill

I have mentioned goodwill in Stage Three, but raise it again as it will often be talked about during negotiations to sell. Valuations are mostly based on a multiple of sustainable earnings or profit. That said, the multiple offered may be increased if the less tangible factors like the accessibility of a patient database, a great reputation, good location, strong staff retention and so on are positive features of the business. These less tangible factors are examples of goodwill.

4.2.4 Selling Equity

Now that you have increased the value, and indeed valued your business, you need to sell it.

Three things are worth considering when you are ready to sell: Who Can Assist You?, Risk Mitigation, and Confidentiality.

Who Can Assist You?

I always advise that you seek the assistance of close contacts/mentors, accountants, those with experience in your industry, and your industry association when you are looking to sell your business. Advisors will ensure you take the best possible path and can be very helpful in negotiations. They will also assist you in the presentation of the business both physically and in the presentation of the crucial accounting numbers. The role you play in the transaction can be anything from fully involved, to nearly completely hands off.

Engaging a business broker is a possible and proven path, but some of the value (usually a large percentage of the sale) will go directly to the broker. The broker will advertise the sale and may have the right contacts that could maximise value. It is worth approaching two or three to compare what is on offer.

Making sure your industry network is aware that your business is up for sale once your staff and practitioners know you have chosen to take this path can also help to find buyers. The timing of the sale might be important to a purchaser, because buying a business in the low billings time of the year (Dec and Jan) is not ideal. Take your time with setting up for a sale before you start looking or advertising the business for sale. This is important as you never know when the opportunity will come, and it is not unrealistic that you may be approached out of the blue.

If you are looking to sell to a larger group network or a corporate entity then, from my experience, such groups are generally looking for:

- High billings, i.e. more than $1 million.
- Good systems — evidence of a system adds value and makes the transition of the business into their operation easier.
- Modern and attractive fit-outs, i.e. not older than five years.
- Good strategic locations — that fit into their current network or plans.
- Clear and easily understood benchmarks and a clean P & L (these matters we have covered earlier).

Having several possible purchasers will create competitive tension and should therefore increase the possibility of a sale. Some years ago, when I was an equity holder in a business named Sports Medicine Centres of Victoria, our group's value was enhanced when a group who had publicly listed their company was looking for a large group business in the eastern states to purchase. Other examples come to mind, such as when a group of practices dominates a particular location, such as the western suburbs of Melbourne, or having a business in a high-growth corridor of a city. Having a practice where you own the building may or may not be an asset. The premises/building has equity value, but the purchaser may not want to buy both your business and your premises. I have been involved in the purchase of such businesses, and we have taken the view to leave the premises in the hands of the owner and rent the promises from them at the commercial rent value. Businesses that can show future growth opportunities, have strong billings (more than $1 million) or have a good rent-to-billings ratio (5% or less) usually sell well. The continuing involvement of the owner is always something to be considered by a purchaser, and it is important to make sure that you are very clear of your intentions with regards to this when you plan to sell your business.

Risk Mitigation

Of course, there are risks with selling your business. I have witnessed both unhappy vendor and unhappy purchaser situations. Such matters can arise when either party is not clear of the other's intentions. I have seen a vendor who remained working in the business that had unreasonable expectations of the new owner. They thought that new equipment or a new fit-out would happen or that they would continue with the same level of authority as they had before. Make sure this does not happen by having very clear expectations before sale. I call this situation the 'unhappy vendor syndrome'. Do not be this person! Similarly, the purchaser may not have fully understood the details of the contract of sale and have differing expectations. The purchaser may have thought you intended to leave at a defined period after the sale or that you would do a certain amount of marketing or mentoring in an unpaid capacity. The above scenarios can be dealt with if all matters are clearly defined before any contract of sale is signed.

If you are an unhappy vendor after the sale, then I suggest you set a date to leave the business. You have hopefully been adequately rewarded with the sale price and the patients you have developed goodwill with who have been transferred to the new owner. If you do decide that you want to continue practising, then you can always establish a new business outside the restraint area.

If you do decide after the sale that you want to continue practising in a similar way, then this may mean that you didn't think through the post-sale situation beforehand. You mightn't have fully prepared for life after the business. I only say this to emphasise that the decision to sell your business is very important and should not be made lightly.

Confidentiality

Both parties to any transactions should be sworn to secrecy. I have seen much disruption to staff and damage to relationships when negotiations are able to be observed or known by staff and practitioners. Your team will be involved in due course, but until a deal is made it should be kept confidential. If nothing happens with that deal, then no one is any the wiser. If necessary, get confidentiality agreements signed by the interested purchaser and only discuss the deal with your close and trusted advisors. "Loose lips sink ships" is a good adage not to follow. Remember, most people see change as a bad thing and almost instantly think they will lose their jobs, which is rarely the case.

4.3 Why is Leveraging Equity Important?

It is important to consider that any asset you have developed and grown over time will be able to be realised as profit for you one day. The money that you receive provides you with choices. It may be part of your retirement fund, or may create an opportunity to explore another business opportunity, or it may allow you to purchase property, or provide you with a more expansive lifestyle. In general, it will create a degree of financial freedom.

Ownership of a business does have an emotional attachment and you need to be prepared to see your efforts passed on to another. This may not be close to mind at the time of sale, but can show up as regret later. Therefore, it is best to be sure when you make the decision and do not take that decision lightly. Be prepared to let go.

I think it is also important to consider those who remain in the business when you sell. You may have already created a succession plan and, if so, certain staff and practitioners may have some expectations that you need to address. They may reasonably expect a reward, either financial or in the creation of a new role in recognition of their efforts in helping you to sell. Creating a handover to the new owner that recognises people and ensures their reasonable expectations are met, so they remain in the business, is important. It can also be rewarding for you as the ex-business owner knowing you have helped your practitioners and staff post sale.

Leveraging equity is a milestone for you because developing or purchasing a business and then selling it at a profit provides great satisfaction and reward for your labours. It will also form part of your legacy and is an achievement you can share with others such as family and friends.

4.4 What Else Do I Need to Leverage Equity?

When you leverage your equity, you need to consider what you will do next. Ideally, you have made plans that are fulfilling and create excitement about your future. You may have negotiated to stay at the business and work in some capacity, either as a practitioner, a mentor, or in some special-purpose role identified by you and the purchaser. You may want to take time away, have a vacation, or consider new investments. If you carefully consider the knowledge and experience you have gained when operating your business, you will realise that you have new skills. You may want to expand those skills by studying business to enable you to enter different industries. You may want to become a consultant or facilitate planning sessions or deliver lectures to various associations. The experience of operating a business, dealing with staff matters, understanding marketing and planning, and having the basic understanding of financial management are all attributes that will serve you well into the future.

In the final chapter of this book, I will detail how the practitioner journey can continue in different ways after you have leveraged your equity. I will explore how others have used the knowledge they harvested to reinvent their careers and create new and exciting pathways.

5.0
HARVESTING KNOWLEDGE

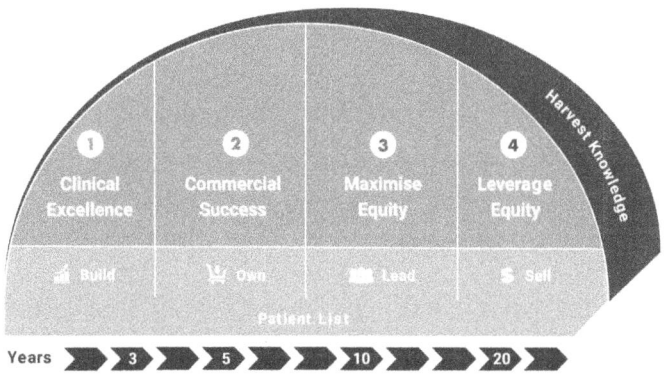

5.1 What is Harvesting Knowledge?

In section 1.4.1 "the law of the farm" was introduced. It is a metaphor that outlines the process of needing to sow a crop in the autumn, tend it, care for it, fertilise and weed it before you harvest the crop in the spring. In other words, there is work to be done to prepare, learn, grow and ultimately achieve key outcomes in your life. Things don't just happen. We don't wake up in the morning and decide we will run a marathon the next day, or decide that we will become a famous actor at our first audition, and so on. This metaphor is a key element behind the concept of harvesting knowledge. When you undertake your journey, you learn, you absorb, you experience, you *read*, and follow others in order to eventually harvest all that knowledge and apply it to new ventures.

Your value as a practitioner resides in your knowledge and not in your job. I have always advised those who I provide consulting to, and to my own children, that having a job is not where your security lies. The knowledge you have and continue to accumulate creates your future opportunities, and people will always employ someone or listen to someone who has such knowledge. You harvest your knowledge when you use this knowledge in a capacity beyond your current working environment.

This concept of harvesting knowledge is not linear, i.e. harvesting knowledge doesn't necessarily need to follow after you have leveraged your list. You may already have a business that you operate and are lecturing, operating a like business, vertically integrating other businesses into your practice business, and so on. So, please do not think that to harvest your knowledge you must follow the journey in the order I have presented in this book.

There are many activities you can pursue after you have leveraged your list, and this section of the book is devoted to highlighting what colleagues or those I have mentored have done with the knowledge they have harvested. My own journey is an example. If you have taken the full journey as I have outlined in this book, then you will have a thorough understanding of your discipline and how to build a career while practising in your profession.

5.2 My Journey

Here is a short description of what I have done to illustrate how I have harvested my knowledge.

I trained as a physiotherapist after learning that my passion to be a world-class athlete was cut short with a career-ending injury at the age of 18 years. I was a high jumper and had recently broken the South Australian open record and won a medal at the Australian championships. It was the injury I sustained that drove me to be involved with the treatment and rehabilitation of track and field athletes and other sportspersons. Upon graduation as a physio, I spent my first year working in a large public hospital in Adelaide, South Australia. Working for a year in a hospital helped me understand more about what my career direction could be without the pressure of moving into private practice as a new graduate. I was lucky enough to meet a mentor, Tony, while working in the hospital. Tony was an enthusiastic and skilled practitioner who had enormous drive. It was Tony who dragged me back from a holiday with an opportunity in the coming months to work at a new sports medicine clinic that was to open in Adelaide, South Australia, called Adelaide Sports Sciences Clinic (ASSC). Upon my return to Adelaide and before the new clinic opened, Tony took me under his wing and, twice weekly, I would attend his clinic where he taught me about knee-injury rehab and post-reconstruction management.

This prepared me well for the new clinic because it exposed me to many injuries from a variety of sports.

Still under Tony's mentoring, I was able to work with new and exciting rehab equipment that the clinic owners had bought into Australia from the USA. I learnt about isokinetic cybex assessment of joints and how to work with fitness professionals to rehabilitate injuries using Nautilus equipment. Working at this clinic helped me understand how to build a list of patients. Little did I know that I would not be in a position to own that list as I would leave South Australia after a year of working at ASSC.

The ASSC experience was invaluable and led to my move to Victoria to work with another committed group of sports medicine professionals. They were the leading sports doctors, podiatrists, dietitians and orthopaedic surgeons in the country and we were working at a clinic named the Malvern Sports Medicine Centre. The environment was intense at this centre and the adage we worked with was that nobody could leave that centre without an anatomical injury diagnosis. This discipline would serve me well working in sports medicine, and the knowledge gained within that environment was invaluable to my progress as a clinician. I gradually built a list of patients and this was assisted by in-house referrals from the other clinicians working in medical, podiatry and other parts of the clinic. Within a few years, I owned a strong list and had regular patients rebooking with new injuries and I was now becoming commercially successful as a practitioner. Harvesting the knowledge of everything I had learnt to this stage of my career, I became an equity partner and eventually a manager of that clinic. Untrained in this capacity, I built up my knowledge by doing and by making sure that if legal or accounting advice was needed, I would reach out to a lawyer or an accountant to learn more. From that single clinic, our core investors and I gradually built a business with a number of other partners from the disciplines of sports medicine, podiatry, physio and accounting. Within 12 years we operated five multidisciplinary sports medicine centres in the Melbourne suburbs, named: Sports Medicine Centres of Victoria (SMCV).

SMCV became known Australia-wide as a hub of excellence. During this time I decreased my clinical load and was working largely unpaid as a manager with that group and growing the centres we had started. The key was that I continued to learn and apply new skills in business operations. That entity was noticed when LifeCare floated on the ASX in Perth in 1999 and their executives visited the eastern states with a view to establishing a foothold in the east. LifeCare made an offer to purchase SMCV in 2000 and we decided that the opportunity was too good to pass up and we sold the business to them.

This opened the door for me to commence a corporate career on the executive team of LifeCare, a listed ASX

Company. That really ramped up my learning and opportunities, as corporate entities owning allied health and sports medicine clinics was a new and emerging corporate activity. The journey for me in the corporate sector was sometimes fraught as I learnt that being a listed public company meant close scrutiny from investors and shareholders, and practices were wary of what life might be like if they divested their business and sold to a corporate. This did not stop practices selling or having their businesses franchised by LifeCare, but it did create some issues to manage when integrating those practices that did decide to sell to or be part of the LifeCare franchise network.

Whilst I was building my knowledge and learning in the corporate environment, I worked steadily on developing my network and connections. I achieved this through my involvement with Sports Medicine Australia, working as a physio in elite sport, volunteering for events and harvesting knowledge from those I met along my journey.

LifeCare was a small corporate entity and struggled to grow quickly enough (a key requirement of being a listed company) and was approached to become part of a larger corporate and subsequently merged with Foundation Health Care (a GP practice aggregator), and that new entity was rebadged as IPN Ltd. A new pathway opened for me as I was now managing general practice medical practices as well as allied health practices.

The CEO of IPN was a fabulous teacher and mentor

and what I learnt from him regarding measurement, performance, recruitment, business development and corporate governance was invaluable. The work was busy and stressful and within two years I felt I was no longer aligned to the business direction and values, so I resigned as an executive from IPN Ltd and took a six-month sabbatical. My story and journey continued with buying and selling businesses, and developing and mentoring both practices and practitioners. I was able to harvest the knowledge I learnt working for IPN in the corporate sector by applying the business principles, developing my mentoring and coaching, further reading of finance and management articles and books, and learning how to share my experience and knowledge with others.

To illustrate the importance of harvesting knowledge in my journey I will list the activities that I have undertaken throughout my journey:

- I established a mentoring and consulting business that is ongoing.
- With some of those I mentored, we started new greenfield multidisciplinary health practices in regional Victoria, where partners are mentoring and developing the skills of young practitioners.
- I was invited to consult, invest and work with a tech start-up called R-U-Ontrak that assists people and providers with injury or with important tasks to plan and achieve their important life goals.

- I was invited by the Board of Sports Medicine Australia (SMA) to step in quickly to assist as interim CEO on two occasions in 2017 and 2019.
- I was invited and set up a clinic in Bali, Indonesia, and still consult to a hospital group in Bali.
- I am working as General Manager at Melbourne Stem Cell Centre Research where we have developed a treatment and research centre treating osteoarthritis with stem cells on the back of establishing a cell-manufacturing supply business, Magellan Stem Cells. We plan to commence a phase-three study with Magellan to identify and gain approval from the regulator for a stem cell product for modifying the disease process with osteoarthritis.
- I was an executive for the International Federation of Sports Medicine from 2008 till 2018 with a goal to further the interests of sports medicine globally.
- I am looking at establishing another consulting business helping professional health association CEOs to grow their skills.
- I have written this book in the hope that I can inspire others to develop their careers and live a work life that is always open to new opportunities.

5.3 What Have Others Done to Harvest Their Knowledge?

Many others have harvested their knowledge and continued to develop themselves and their careers, which I have followed and hopefully assisted.

Lyn Watson: Shoulder Specialist

I met Lyn Watson as a recent graduate when she came to work at SMCV. Lyn was an enthusiastic therapist who enrolled in every course that was being conducted at the time and spent her weekends watching surgeons operate if she was not attending a course.

One day she approached me and advised that she believed that the current methods for treating shoulders were flawed and she was working on a new approach. She had also identified a surgeon to work with and a new paradigm for shoulder treatment, and rehab was created with that surgeon. This subsequently became a unique and effective approach that would see many patients in their sixties and seventies able to continue their golf, tennis and swimming when shoulder pain had previously denied them these activities.

Not long afterwards, Lyn was conducting courses in Australia and then overseas where her methods, supported by her leading research, were being adopted widely. This was at a time when the line of professional sportspersons with shoulder pain became longer and longer and included world champions and record makers in many sports. At this time Lyn developed her 'shoulder team' of clinicians working with her and her private practice thrived.

Lyn harvested her knowledge by combining clinical work, teaching her team, and establishing a business lecturing and presenting courses. This saw her reputation grow and her influence extend widely.

Lyn is indeed an example of what one can do with their passion, their hard work, and their persistence when they apply that to new business models to create new pathways for the treatment of complex problems.

Lyn continues to harvest her knowledge by introducing others into the business opportunities she has created. Lyn has achieved all this while raising a family, treating her patients, mentoring and developing others, and retaining the same joy she exhibited as a young and aspiring clinician.

Matt Appleton: Podiatrist

Matt started working with my group as a clinical podiatrist. Matt quickly took on partners and established a brand called Sportspods, which he developed, soon establishing podiatry practices within SMCV. Matt had an impressive approach to musculoskeletal podiatry and developed a reputation with his group as a leader in assessment and treatment for sports-related foot pathology. Within no time, he established an orthotic company that supplied custom-made devices to his clients and to the broader podiatric community. The vertical integration of his business continued with the establishment of boutique sports shoe shops branded Active Feet, dedicated to the best and most appropriate footwear for active people in sport and recreation. Matt achieved all this while working under the umbrella of SMCV. In fact, Matt and I were key parties in the corporate negotiations on behalf of SMCV's medical and allied health partners.

Matt continues to consult part-time and his brand has become supplying these consulting services, as he has sold his orthotic supply company and shoe stores. Matt's story illustrates how applying the core skills learnt as a clinician, with the addition of sound principles, can be leveraged, or harvested, to develop a number of different businesses that can thrive and provide great satisfaction within a clinical practice. He certainly has harvested his knowledge well.

Dr Jon Ford: Low Back Pain and Functional Restoration

Jon Ford arrived as a new graduate also at Prahran Sports Medicine Centre in 1995 (which became LifeCare Prahran Sports medicine in 2000). Jon quickly established himself as a busy and very effective practitioner. One day he came to me and said that he wanted to develop a career treating compensable low back pain problems. He had developed a rapport with a rehabilitation facility and asked if he could use a space in the clinic to explore concepts and practise a new type of therapy with selected patients.

He developed a functional restoration program for treating chronic low back disorders who had mostly failed with conventional treatments. He identified that hands-on treatment was no longer effective with such patients and led to therapist-patient dependence. He worked hard, often seeing only two or three patients in a morning, spending long periods of time with each patient exploring how he could develop programs for them as individuals to work on by themselves and other programs to work on in a group environment. He expanded his team of clinicians to include occupational psychologists and pain physicians as well as carefully selected physios. His work became full-time and he established Spinal Management Clinics of Victoria and operated a series of practices under the umbrella of SMCV. Jon achieved his PhD and that enhanced his reputation further, and since that time he has fostered many others into PhD programs.

Jon's Spinal Management entity was eventually purchased by LifeCare in the early 2000s and he built the team for LifeCare that worked across Victoria in multidisciplinary pain practices treating and rehabilitating those with chronic low back pain problems. Jon eventually left LifeCare and moved his team and practices into a new entity called Advance Healthcare that he still operates today.

Jon is a good example of another clinician who followed

his passion and worked on his craft with little financial reward early in his career as he harvested knowledge. He worked closely with me and we learnt many business principles together working in the corporate environment. We established a venture together called Knowledge and Learning Solutions International and operated that business for some years. That business was established to provide online learning modules and education to a variety of disciplines in allied health and pain medicine. This business is a great example of how both Jon and I harvested our knowledge together.

Andrew Wallis: The Sporting Hip and Groin

Andrew trained in South Australia and landed in Melbourne in the early 2000s, as he wished to develop his career in elite sport and the opportunities in South Australia were limited due to the smaller number of elite teams. He came to work at LifeCare Prahran Sports Medicine where he quickly established himself as a leading therapist with a keen interest in lower limb injuries.

Working in multidisciplinary sports medicine afforded Andrew the opportunity to meet clinicians from different disciplines and it was a sports physician who recommended Andrew for a role at St Kilda football club (a professional team in the Australian Football League). Andrew's reputation grew, as did his interest in hip and groin pain. He started lecturing and conducting courses in hip and groin pathology and dysfunction. He became well known with this and elite athletes began seeking him out from clubs across Australia.

Andrew became an equity partner with me in a new multidisciplinary sports medicine business where he developed a team of clinicians who worked under his direction, seeing his patients under his guidance, and gradually developing their own specific expertise. His team grew as did his practice. So well regarded was Andrew, that he decided to sell his equity as he was approached by a prominent orthopaedic group to work with them and lead a clinic for them. He is now an equity holder in that business and continues to conduct courses in the management and treatment of hip and groin injuries and pathologies across Australia.

Like Lyn, Andrew has retained his passion for treating patients, for sharing his knowledge and growing a team around him. By studying and reading, being mentored by orthopaedic surgeons and leading practitioners, and with a focus on treating patients in a specialist area of injury management, Andrew has harvested this knowledge to teach and train others and develop a successful business in the process.

*

Those whom I have featured above are just a few of the

clinicians whose journeys I know well. They all exhibited very similar traits personally and in practice. They worked hard and diligently to become excellent clinicians who were commercially successful. That was their start, but they also understood the importance of continuing to learn, choosing mentors wisely, sharing their knowledge, and mentoring others. Their enthusiasm, positivity and experiences enabled them to build high-functioning teams of people who worked with them and for them. Their vision to do more and grow their careers was also a clear similarity. They truly harvested their knowledge to build multiple opportunities outside of their regular working environments to create satisfying, fulfilling and outstanding careers with high regard from their peers, their patients, and those whom they assisted in their careers.

APPENDICES

1. Achieving your Career Objectives (ACO)

Independent practitioners need ongoing mentoring/reviews to assist them in improving their clinical excellence and developing their practices. This review is designed to assist you to achieve your short- and long-term objectives and therefore we ask that you carefully consider your responses to ensure maximum benefit is achieved.

ACO Review is made up of the following:

Section A: Reviewing Performance
Section B: Setting Short-/Medium-Term Objectives
Section C: Practise Self-Assessment
Section D: Setting Long-Term Objectives

If this is your **first ACO review**, please complete Sections B and C as a means of setting objectives, methods and KPIs for the next review.

For those **having already done an ACO review**, please ensure you incorporate the information from Sections B and C from your previous review into Section A of this review.

The ACO should be completed by the practitioner in preparation for the annual review meeting with your Commercial Mentor.

Documents for Illustrative Purposes Only

Please type only in the grey text boxes or check boxes.

Name:

Position:

Practice:

Date of this ACO discussion:

Date of last ACO discussion:

Name of Commercial Mentor:

Signed (Practitioner):

1. Achieving your Career Objectives (ACO)

Section A: Reviewing Performance

Insert 12-month objectives, methods and KPIs from last ACO review, the Quarterly Practitioner Review or from informal objectives discussed with your Commercial Mentor over the last period. This information should be inserted before the ACO review meeting.

Performance Objectives	Methods of Achieving Objectives	Key Performance Indicator (KPI)	KPI Achieved
Example: • To bill $15,000 per month for the last 3 months of the financial year	Example: • Write to the GP of every patient I see • Focus on Patient Management principles for every patient	Example: • $/practitioner hour of $110 • 34 hours per month • 40% of referrals direct	Yes/No
Clinical			
Commercial and revenue-generating			

Performance Objectives	Methods of Achieving Objectives	Key Performance Indicator (KPI)	KPI Achieved
Risk management (e.g. contracts, complaints, OH&S, work/life balance)			
Administration (e.g. completing referrer tracker, service standards, compensable body paperwork)			
Research/postgraduate			
Total score of KPI achieved/KPI not achieved			

Section A (Continued): Scoring Performance

Feedback on level of performance against objectives in the period under review.

To be completed by the practitioner's Commercial Mentor.

1. Achieving your Career Objectives (ACO)

Assessing Individual Practitioner Performance

Rating:

Comments:

Rating Scale

Outstanding — Demonstration of performance consistently exceeding expectations. The consistently high standard has earned recognition by others internal and/or external to the practice.

Good — Overall demonstration of consistent and sustained performance with all objectives being met and some being exceeded.

Satisfactory — Performance in most areas met the requirements of the position whilst others missed by a small margin.

Unsatisfactory — Performance and/or behaviour falls short of the required standard.

Section B: Setting Short-/Medium-Term Objectives

To be drafted by the practitioner prior to and then jointly agreed with the Commercial Mentor at the ACO meeting. Objectives are Specific, Measurable, Achievable, Realistic, Timebound (SMART).

Objectives	Methods of Achieving Objectives	Key Performance Indicator (KPI)
Example • To bill $15,000 per month for the last 3 months of the financial year	Example • Write to the GP of every patient I see • Focus on Patient Management principles for every patient	Example • $/practitioner hour of $110 • 34 hours per month • 40% of referrals direct
Clinical		
Commercial and revenue-generating		
Risk management		

1. Achieving your Career Objectives (ACO)

Objectives	Methods of Achieving Objectives	Key Performance Indicator (KPI)
Administration (e.g. referrer tracker, RM spreadsheet)		
Research/postgraduate		

Section C: Self-Assessment

Habits Of Highly Successful Practitioners

Please answer the following questions as a means of evaluating your commercial behaviours. Do you:

Question	Comments
Ever turn a patient away? Always Sometimes Rarely Never	
Have spots to grow? Always Sometimes Rarely Never	
Have a strategy in place with reception for fitting people in? Yes No Not sure	
See new patients the next day? Always Sometimes Rarely Never	
Provide "Intensive Care"? Always Sometimes Rarely Never	
What is your ratio of new to subsequent treatments? 1:7 or more 1:5 1:3 1:1 or less	
Know how every new patient is referred to you Always Sometimes Rarely Never	
Write or call referrers: Day 1? Always Sometimes Rarely Never	
Write or call referrers: Fortnightly? Always Sometimes Rarely Never	
Write or call referrers: On discharge? Always Sometimes Rarely Never	

1. Achieving your Career Objectives (ACO)

Question	Comments
Introduce yourself to local GPs? > 7 5 2 No	
Keep a register of Local GPs? Yes No	
Have a marketing plan written down? Yes No	
Write to a patient's GP/surgeon to let them know about their patient, even if they are not the referrer? Always Sometimes Rarely Never	
Measure your patient numbers? Always Sometimes Rarely Never	
Provide a reliable service? Always Sometimes Rarely Never	
Set patient expectations? Always Sometimes Rarely Never	
Provide a padded face hole? Always Sometimes Rarely Never	
Provide a clean face sheet for the face hole on the plinth? Always Sometimes Rarely Never	
Walk your patient after treatment to reception? Always Sometimes Rarely Never	
Dress to Impress? Always Sometimes Rarely Never	
Meet with respect? Always Sometimes Rarely Never	

Question	Comments
Apologise if late? Always Sometimes Rarely Never	
Make sure your cubicle is tidy? Always Sometimes Rarely Never	
Make sure your treatment area is tidy? Always Sometimes Rarely Never	
Ensure everyone leaves with something, e.g. exercise sheet? Always Sometimes Rarely Never	
Ensure everyone leaves feeling better than on arrival? Always Sometimes Rarely Never	
Specify the day you next need to see them? Always Sometimes Rarely Never	
Ask the patient to "Please call me if anything is wrong"? Always Sometimes Rarely Never	
Recognise Critical Service Moments? Always Sometimes Rarely Never	
Take ownership of any problems and fix them? Always Sometimes Rarely Never	
Remember and use the patient's name? Always Sometimes Rarely Never	
Actively address any additional problems they raise? Always Sometimes Rarely Never	
Tell the patient if you spend extra time with them? Always Sometimes Rarely Never	
Patient call backs (e.g. if cancelled or did not attend) Always Sometimes Rarely Never	

1. Achieving your Career Objectives (ACO)

Question	Comments
Proactively use any "down time"? Always Sometimes Rarely Never	
Look at personal email? Daily Weekly Monthly Never	
Look at social media? Daily Weekly Monthly Never	
Transfer patient trust when going on holidays? Always Sometimes Rarely Never	

Section D: Long-Term Objectives

Practice objectives to be achieved Mid range (around 2 years)	Method to achieve objective
Practice objectives to be achieved Long range (around 5 years)	Method to achieve objective

ACO Review: A Guide to Completion

The Achieving your Career Objectives (ACO) Review is a critical component of assisting practitioners to achieve their potential in the short- and long-term. Following is a guide to completing an ACO review to assist practitioners and Commercial Mentors.

The process for completing an ACO Review is as follows:
- Annual reminder to practitioners to complete an ACO Review received (more frequent review may occur if deemed necessary by the practitioner/Commercial Mentor).
- Practitioner reviews previous year's Review and in particular the goals set.

- Practitioner completes the Review for the current year with reference to the goals from the previous period. Even if a formal Review has not occurred, this evaluation of performance can occur based on less formally determined goals.
- Practitioner arranges a time to meet the Commercial Mentor to discuss the review where feedback, scoring of performance and modifications to the document are made.

In completing (the Practitioner) or discussing (the Commercial Mentor) an ACO Review, the following points may wish to be considered.

Goals and KPIs *must* be measurable. For ideas about specific goals, previous versions of the Quarterly Practitioner Review should be studied (e.g. $ per hour, average hours, total revenue, percentage of direct referrals, number of referrals per month, etc).

As a rule it is best to start with longer-term goals, i.e. five years plus. Think honestly and with consideration as to where you truly want to be in five years' time. Consider:
- How much you want to earn.
- How many hours per week you want to work.
- The proportion of those hours spent working clinically versus non-clinically (e.g. business, academic, consulting, etc), doing different types of work (e.g. Pilates, sports, consulting).
- Be specific about which practices.

Think also about what drives you as a professional and how these drivers fit within the practice values.

Think about how these drivers impact upon your long-term goals.

Once you have determined these things, you can work backwards to your mid-term goals and annual goals. For example, many practitioners express the desire to have equity in a practice based on a desire to earn $100,000. However, it is perfectly feasible to earn this figure without equity working as a practitioner.

Think of an ACO Review as an opportunity to communicate your needs so that your Commercial Mentor can work as hard as possible at meeting them.

Any further queries about completing an ACO Review should be discussed with your Commercial Mentor.

2. Achieving your Business Objectives (ABO)

Documents for Illustrative Purposes Only

Key leaders in any private practice business (e.g. Practice Manager, Principal Practitioner, equity holders) should review performance on an annual basis.

ABO Review is made up of the following:

Section A:	Reviewing Practice Performance
Section B:	Historical Data
Section C:	Setting 12-Month Objectives
Section D:	Relationship Marketing and Business Development Plan
Section E:	Long-Term Practice Objectives

If this is the practice's **first ABO review**, please complete Sections C and D as a means of setting objectives, methods and KPIs for the next review.

For practices **having already done an ABO review**, please ensure the information from Sections C and D from the previous review is inserted into Sections A and B of this review.

The ABO should be completed by the Practice Principal ± Equity Holder in preparation for the annual review meeting with the practice Commercial Mentor.

2. Achieving your Business Objectives (ABO)

Practice Name:

Practice Manager:

Equity Program/Senior Practitioner (if appropriate):

Date of this ABO discussion:

Date of last ABO discussion:

Name of Commercial Mentor
(if role exists, otherwise Business Equity Holder):

Signed (Business Equity Holder):

Section A: Reviewing Practice Performance

Insert 12-month objectives for the practice, methods and KPIs from last ABO review, or from informal objectives discussed over the last period. This information should be inserted before the ABO review meeting.

Practice Performance Objectives	Methods of Achieving Objectives	Key Performance Indicator (KPI)	KPI Achieved
Example: • To attain a $/practitioner hour of $140	Example: • Fully implement the LDoctor Marketing Protocol • Engage the services of a medical specialist as a subtenant	Example: • Achieve 30 visits to medical practices • Physio annual billings of $...K	Yes/No
Commercial and revenue-generating, billing and commercial targets (e.g. physio, doctor, podiatry, other)			
RISK — equipment, WHS insurances, etc			
Practitioner (e.g. mentoring, clinical support, research/postgrad)			

2. Achieving your Business Objectives (ABO)

Practice Performance Objectives	Methods of Achieving Objectives	Key Performance Indicator (KPI)	KPI Achieved
Administration staff (e.g. retention, service standards, culture, hours, processes)			
Total score of KPI achieved/KPI not achieved			SCORE

Scoring Achieving Objectives

Feedback on level of achieving objective against objectives in the period under review.

To be completed by the Practice Principal ± Equity Holder.

Assessing Overall Business Achieving Objective

Rating:

Comments:

Rating Scale

Outstanding — Demonstration of achieving objective consistently exceeding expectations. The consistently high standard has earned recognition by others internal and/or external to the business.

Good — Overall demonstration of consistent and sustained achieving objective with all objectives being met and some being exceeded.

Satisfactory — Achieving objective in most areas met the requirements of the position whilst others missed by a small margin.

Unsatisfactory — Achieving objective and/or behaviour falls short of the required standard.

Section B: Historical Data

Understanding the history of a practice is critical to knowing the way forward. The following table should be completed. This data set should encompass the past two financial years in addition to the coming financial year to measure your business's progress over a three-year period. This is helpful because potential purchases are interested in three years of financial data.

Financial Year	Figures/ DATA	Data source	Comments on key issues for the financial year
• Insert Financial Year • Practice budget revenue • Practice actual revenue • Profit budget • Profit actual • Practice costs (%)			
• Insert Financial Year • Practice budget revenue • Practice actual revenue • Profit budget • Profit actual • Practice costs (%)			

Financial Year	Figures/ DATA	Data source	Comments on key issues for the financial year
• Insert Financial Year • Practice budget revenue • Practice actual revenue • Profit budget • Profit actual • Practice costs (%)			

Section C: Setting 12-Month Objectives

To be drafted by the Practice Principal ± Equity Holder in preparation for review by the Commercial Mentor. Performance objectives are Specific, Measurable, Achievable, Realistic, Timebound (SMART).

Practice Performance Objectives	Methods of Achieving Objectives	Key Performance Indicator (KPI)
Commercial objectives (e.g. achieve billings to achieve budget, practitioner costs, property, admin costs, new services, etc)		
Example: • To attain a $/practitioner hour of $140	Example: • Fully implement the LCH Doctor Marketing Protocol • Engage the services of a medical specialist as a subtenant	Example: • Achieve 30 visits to medical practices • Physio annual billings of $80K
Risk management (e.g. contracts, complaints, OH+S, facilities, maintenance, work/life balance, retention, key leader discussions)		

Practice Performance Objectives	Methods of Achieving Objectives	Key Performance Indicator (KPI)
Practitioner (e.g. mentoring, clinical, career development, discipline liaison, research/postgrad)		
Administration staff (e.g. retention, service standards, culture, business budget/objective understanding)		

Section D: Relationship Marketing and Business Development Plan

It is important for the business to outline plans to develop and market the business.

Marketing target	Methods	Resources required	KPI
e.g. new referrers, online appts, digital approach and socials, old clients follow-up, sports club affiliations	Identify who via referrer trackers, create content for socials, review technology options, EDMs	Budget for activity, designate person to implement, plan timing of activities	Measure performance with binary yes/no approach
Insert marketing target 1 (e.g. number of new clients)	Insert methods specific to the marketing target (e.g. mail-out new patient letter within 7 days)	Insert resources required (e.g. fridge magnets)	Insert quantifiable target for each method (e.g. insert a target number for this activity)

Section E: Practice Self-Assessment

Habits of Highly Successful Practitioners and Customer Service

Please answer the following questions as a means of evaluating clinical and commercial behaviours of the practitioners at your practice. Please tick relevant box and add comments.

Question	Comments
Do your practitioners ever turn a patient away? Always Sometimes Rarely Never	
Do you have spots to grow? Always Sometimes Rarely Never	
Do you have a strategy in place with reception for fitting people in? Yes No Not sure	
Do you see new acute patients the next day? Always Sometimes Rarely Never	
Do you provide "intensive care"? Always Sometimes Rarely Never	
What is your ratio of New to Subsequent treatments? 1:7 or more 1:5 1:3 1:1 or less	
Do you know how every new patient is referred to you? Always Sometimes Rarely Never	

2. Achieving your Business Objectives (ABO)

Question	Comments
Do you write or call referrers: • Day 1? Always Sometimes Rarely Never	
Do you write or call referrers: • Fortnightly? Always Sometimes Rarely Never	
Do you write or call referrers: • On discharge? Always Sometimes Rarely Never	
Have you introduced yourself to a local GP? more than 7 5 2 no	
Do you keep a register of Local GPs? Yes No	
Do You Have A Marketing Plan Written Down? Yes No	
Do you write to a patient's GP/surgeon to let them know about their patient, even if they are not the referrer? Daily Weekly Monthly Never	
Do you measure your patient numbers? Daily Weekly Monthly Never	
Do you provide a reliable service? Always Sometimes Rarely Never	
Do you set their expectations? Always Sometimes Rarely Never	
Provide a padded face hole? Always Sometimes Rarely Never	

Question	Comments
Provide a clean face sheet for the face hole on the plinth? Always Sometimes Rarely Never	
Do you walk your patient to the reception desk? Always Sometimes Rarely Never	
Do you dress to impress? Always Sometimes Rarely Never	
Do you meet with respect? Always Sometimes Rarely Never	
Do you apologise if late? Always Sometimes Rarely Never	
Do you make sure your cubicle is tidy? Always Sometimes Rarely Never	
Do you make sure your treatment area is tidy? Always Sometimes Rarely Never	
Do you ensure everyone leaves with something? Always Sometimes Rarely Never	
Ensure everyone leaves feeling better Always Sometimes Rarely Never	
Tell the patient to "Please call me if anything is wrong" Always Sometimes Rarely Never	
Recognise Critical Service Moments Always Sometimes Rarely Never	

2. Achieving your Business Objectives (ABO)

Question	Comments
Take ownership of any problems and fix them Always　　Sometimes　　Rarely　　Never	
Remember & use patient's name Always　　Sometimes　　Rarely　　Never	
Actively address any additional problems patients raise Always　　Sometimes　　Rarely　　Never	
Tell patients if you spend extra time with them Always　　Sometimes　　Rarely　　Never	
Patient call backs Always　　Sometimes　　Rarely　　Never	
Proactively use any "Down Time" Always　　Sometimes　　Rarely　　Never	
Look at personal email Daily　　Weekly　　Monthly　　Never	
Do you look at social media while at work Daily　　Weekly　　Monthly　　Never	
Transfer trust when going on holidays Always　　Sometimes　　Rarely　　Never	

Section E: Long-Term Business Objectives

Business objectives to be achieved e.g. improve staff retention, improve productivity with technology, relationship development, new services, etc Mid range (around 2 years)	**Method to achieve objective**
Practice objectives to be achieved e.g. new equity partners, revenue increase, new premises Long range (around 5 years)	**Method to achieve objective**

ABO Review: A Guide to Completion

The Achieving your Business Objectives (ABO) Review is a critical component to assist the business to achieve its potential in the short- and long-term.

The process for completing an ABO Review is as follows:

* Annual reminder to complete an ABO Review received (more frequent review may occur if deemed necessary by the Commercial Mentor).
* Practice Principal ± Equity Holder reviews previous year's Review and in particular the goals set.
* Practice Principal ± Equity Holder completes the Review for the current year with reference to the goals from the previous period.
* Practice Principal ± Equity Holder arranges a time to meet the Commercial Mentor to discuss the review where feedback, scoring of performance and modifications to the document are made.

In completing (the Practice Principal ± Equity Holder) or discussing (the Commercial Mentor) an ABO Review, the following points should be considered:

Goals and KPIs *must* be measurable. Examples of this are provided in the ABO Review template. For ideas about specific goals previous versions of the KPIs (e.g. $ per hour, average hours, total revenue, percentage of direct referrals, number of referrals per month, etc). Goals should be global and also specific to service lines (e.g. doctor, physio, massage) and, if necessary, practitioners.

An ABO Review is an opportunity to set clear objectives for the business. This is in the best interest of practitioners as it will assist them to be more productive and engaged.

Acknowledgements

During Covid lockdown I decided that the book I had thought about, made many notes for, and viewed as a passion project should be written!

I had put to paper some elements of this book in conjunction with my partner at LifeCare, Dr Jon Ford. It was after chatting with our social media consultant, Mr Andy Ford, and the PR consultant at my stem-cell venture, Mr Seamus Bradley, that I decided to meet with Andy and his business's recently appointed book editor, Chris Grierson, to discuss the process for creating and publishing this book. Andy and Chris sat me down and advised me to work out what voice I should use to write the book. They encouraged me to discipline myself to spend some four months with them workshopping the structure of the book. The words of Chris resonated: "Do not just lift material from what you already have written, start at the beginning and write your book sequentially based on the structure we have worked with you to create!" I took this sound advice. I thank and acknowledge Andy and Chris, particularly for Chris's patience, drive and persistence with reviews and advice.

I am indebted to many others who have helped me. To Paul Coburn and Jon Ford for reading the manuscript and providing great feedback. To those who also read and generously agreed to endorse the book, I thank you: Trish Wisbey-Roth, Cris Massis and Professor Peter Brukner. A big shout-out to Professor Karim M. Khan who wrote the foreword as well as providing some very valuable insights to improve the manuscript.

Many others have inspired me over my career and in that way contributed to the book, as did those whom I mentored and became mentors to me! To Tony Williamson who taught me many life lessons and many truisms like "Write it down, Mike" when he saw that I had a good idea.

In my early days entering the business of healthcare, my dear friend David A. Hickinbotham introduced me to new authors and to the work of Stephen R. Covey. David, I thank you.

I also acknowledge some special people that hopefully I assisted on their journeys as they were also partners in my journey: Lyn Watson, Andrew Wallis and Matthew Appleton.

Finally, the biggest thankyou goes to my wife Sarah Jane Watson and our children Sebastian, Madelaine, Lucinda and Charlie who inspire me every day.

Michael Kenihan

About the Author

Michael Kenihan is a legend in the Australian allied health community. Over four decades, Michael has excelled as a sports physiotherapist, business manager, sports administrator, entrepreneur, coach and thought leader in the health and sports medicine sectors.

It is fair to say that Michael understands the full spectrum of the health practitioner's journey, given his extensive credentials, which include being a Fellow of Sports Medicine Australia, experience running Australia's largest allied health network LifeCare (with major acquisitions and divestitures, including an IPO), creating several start-up health businesses, such as Melbourne Stem Cell Centre and technology application R-U-Ontrak.

His own journey demonstrates that he lives his ethos, successfully maintaining his work-life balance, having raised four children with his wife Sarah Jane whilst both having busy careers.

After coaching many leaders in the field, Michael wrote *The Health Practitioner's Journey* as a way to consolidate his knowledge and pass on this know-how to the next generations of health practitioners, enabling them to follow his four-stage coaching process to maximise their careers and finances. As Michael likes to say: the ability to listen and learn from others is the key to personal and professional success.

You can connect with Michael via his website: michaelkenihan. com.au

Index

A's, Three - Ability, Affability, Availability 54, 62-63

Behaviours, essential
- be on time 45
- change the patient 45
- count and measure 44
- never decline a patient 42
- next-day treatment 43
- set patient expectations 45
- thank referrer 45
- transfer trust 45

Benchmarks, expenditure 190

Bluffing 46

Branding
- business 156-158
- personal 97-98

Business
- assets 218-221
- benchmarks 190
- finance 131
- goodwill 223
- growing 170-176
- induction 178
- managing 176-202
- measuring 188-196
- mentoring 180
- recruitment 178
- reporting 190-196
- systems and policies 164-165, 221
- training 179

Business, greenfield 138-169
- branding 156-158
- checklist 150-156
- core competencies 143-145
- location 146
- mission 143
- planning 139-140
- premises and fit-out 158-164
- pricing 165-167
- starting 149
- systems and policies 164-165, 221
- vision 142

CAPEX 148

Care plan 87

Cialdini, Robert, Influence, The Psychology of Persuasion, 80, 83

Circle of Influence 78-79
Circle of Concern 78-79

Clinical excellence 18-65
- achieving 56-64
- benefits of 55
- conferences 95
- courses 95

- definition 18
- developing (stage 2) 95-97
- effectiveness, efficiency 40-41
- reading 95
- teaching 96
- volunteering 96

Clinical reasoning 18
- SOAP Subjective, Objective, Assessment, Plan & Treatment 18
- application 28
    action and behaviours 30-31
    advice and messaging 28
    therapy 29-30

Communication model 41

Consultation 23
- closing consultation 27
- customisation of benefits 25
- expectations, engineered and managed 26, 27
- further information provided to patient 26
- instilling confidence 26
- preparation 22
- rapport building 22, 27
- reassessment 26, 30
- scheduling next consultation

Consultants 201-202

Covey, Steven, The Seven Habits of Highly Effective People 35, 58, 75, 77, 78, 150

Development, personal and professional 33-34

Due diligence 132

EBITDA 126-127

Effectiveness/Efficiency 40

Eight steps of selling 20-28

Emotional bank account 75-77

Empathy 29, 54

Engagement model 15-17

Equity
- benefits 202
- debts and liabilities 217
- defintion 214
- importance of 228
- leveraging 214
- maximising 124, 202-206
- selling 224
- sharing 180
- valuing 222

Expectations 24, 27, 30, 45, 46-48, 130, 173, 174

Feedback 186-188

Fees 165-167

Goal setting 36-40
- clinical, commercial, risk management, administration, research 39
- quantative, qualitative 38

Goodwill 223

Index

Insurance 39, 102, 135, 138, 197, 217

Jargon, avoid 28

Knowledge, harvesting 231-247

KPI's 99
- administration 101
- assessing 133
- binary 99
- career development 102-103
- clinical activities 99
- commercial improvement 100
- in reviews 188
- setting 37

Leadership 197-198

List
- building 11-64 (see clinical excellence)
- leading 119-206
- owning 65-116
- selling 207-250

List, leading 119-206
- accreditation 135
- balance sheet, review 136
- contract of sale 136-137
- due diligence 132
- financing 131
- insurance 135
- owning the business 119
- P&L reports 132
- price, considerations 125-131
- See Equity

List, owning 71-74
- Circle of Concern 77-80
- Circle of Influence 77-80
- emotional bank account (EBA) 75-77
- persuasion 80-84
  authority 81
  commitment, consistency 82
  liking 83
  reciprocation 80, 81
  scarcity 82
  social proof 83-84
- referrer relationship building 84-94
  acknowledge referrer 91
  communicate with referrers 91
  risks that the referrer takes 87-89
  strategic relationships 89-91
- strategies 74

List, selling 207-250
- assets 218-223
- client database 219
- confidentiality 227-228
- debts and liabilities 217
- harvesting knowledge 231-247
- presentation 216
- premises 217
- reasons for 207-214
See Equity

Listening 22, 23, 54, 112-114, 115-116

Made-to-stick messaging 92

Managing
- facility 177
- induction 178-179
- mentoring 180
- performance leadership 185-188
- recruiting 177-178
- retention 180-181
- training 179

Marketing, communication 171-172

Marketing plan 103-109

Marketing plan for practitioners 174

Mental health referral 25

Mentoring 32-33, 180

Messaging 28, 29

MK's 19 Laws of Growth 173-176

Networking 49, 206

Next-day treatment 44

OPEX 148

Patience 58-59

Patient relationship building 74-84

Patient
- compliance 31
- finding new 171
- requests 116

Performance leadership 185

Performance review 187-188

Porter's Five Forces 140

Pricing 165-167

Productivity 14-17
benefits of 17

Professionalism 54

Profitability 125-127

Punctuality 45

Rescheduling 43

Referrer
- creating 49
- database 174, 188
- gifts 91
- identifying 104
- maintaining relationship 108
- relationship building 84-92
- thanking 45, 49
- top 10 133
- tracking 39, 73

Relationship marketing 50-54
- Ladder of Loyalty 52

Relationships, strategic 172

Risk
- management 196-197
- mitigation 226-227

RMBD (Relationship marketing business development) 93-94

Service, personalised 54, 76

SOAP approach 19

Success, commercial
- definition 70
- importance of, opportunities it brings 109-111

Succession planning 198-200

Supply and demand 167-169

Training 32-34
- clinical mentors 32
- courses 34
- development, personal and professional 33
- observation 33
- volunteering 34

Treatment
- count and measure 44
- progressing 30
- reassessing 31
- review plan 50

Tidy up 49

Time management 34-35, 47-50, 101, 112, 140, 179
- catch up 50
- matrix 35
- review patient plans 50
- ring a client 48
- ring a referrer 48
- ring an employer 50
- tidy up 49
- visit a sports club 49

Trust
- importance of 22, 30, 31
- transfer 48
- developing 58, 82

Under-promise, over-deliver 24, 31

Unique selling proposition (USP) 63-64, 69-70, 96-97, 145, 175

Unit trust 137, 182-183, 193

Work environment
- empowered 57-60
- extrinsic factors 59-60
- intrinsic factors 56-59

www.ingramcontent.com/pod-product-compliance
Lightning Source LLC
Chambersburg PA
CBHW062031290426
44109CB00026B/2594